Get Your Freight Broker License from the Federal Government

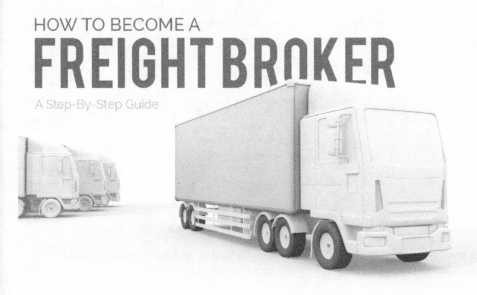

HOW TO BECOME A
FREIGHT BROKER
A Step-By-Step Guide

Freight Brokers Keep the Economy Running

Author: Milton Collier

Mr. Collier graduated from Strayer University with a Bachelor of Business Administration & Business Management Degree. Worked in Management, Leadership and Ownership roles with some of the largest Transportation and Logistical Companies in the World, such as DHL, FedEx, Roadrunner and Swift with extensive experience and successful track record in the Transportation and Logistics Industry.

Mr. Milton L. Collier was the #1 Revenue and Profit Producer for DHL Freight. Established Millions of Dollars Book of Business and Earned High Six Figure Income. DHL is one of the Largest Logistical Companies in the World, serving over 220 countries.

Mr. Collier is a Master Freight Broker, Retired Military Veteran and Business Owner. He's one of the Best Trainers in the Freight Brokerage Industry and teach Freight Brokers a proven system and provide a road map towards success in transportation brokering, from experts in the field! No matter the state of the economy, products will always need to be shipped.

Book Introduction: (Getting Your Freight Broker License)

Overview

Learn the skills you need to be a successful Freight Broker. This is a growing industry of licensed individuals or corporations that help make a shipper and an authorized motor carrier successful in the transporting of freight.

Let's GET your Freight Broker License:

It's a great time to be in the freight brokering business, and there are plenty of reasons to consider starting your own brokerage now.

With an improving economy across the U.S., an increasingly stable and growing industry, and increasing demand for new brokers, you have all the external conditions to become a successful freight broker.

We've compiled this comprehensive guide and an infographic that will take you through the main steps of launching your business.

What you need to know before you become a freight broker

Before you take the first steps to launching your freight brokerage, it's a good idea to review the role of the broker in the industry.

Besides earning well – freight brokers can make up to $100,000 per year – they're also indispensable for the transportation of goods and cargo. Essentially, freight brokers keep the economy running.

What does a freight broker do?

Freight brokers are filling in a crucial role in the movement of freight, as the missing link between shippers and carriers. They negotiate good shipping rates and fast deliveries from transportation companies, and connect them with the businesses that need to transport goods or cargo, so carriers can maximize their loads.

Besides acting as an intermediary, brokers have an important function in the tracking of freight, as they keep thorough records of pickups and deliveries, and other information. They also oversee the legal part of the transportation, as they need to be experts in shipping regulations and procedures.

Brokers are the ones who make sure that each step of the transportation process occurs, so that the freight arrives safely to its final destination. To become a freight broker for trucking and transportation means to take responsibility for a vital part of the shipping process.

Freight Broker Journey

Starting your freight brokering journey does not need to be complicated – but you do need to prepare thoroughly for launching a freight brokerage business.

So what does it take to become the much-needed middleman in the transportation industry?

Steps to becoming a freight broker......

1. Gain Industry Training and Experience

1.1. Refresh or Develop Some General Skills

While brokering freight does require knowledge and experience in the field, there is nothing you cannot gain with practice and diligence. In other words, a strong will is among the most important qualities you need to have in order to make it.

In terms of skills, it's a good idea to refresh your math skills because you'll need to make use of them on a daily basis. Turning on your business know-how is important too, because you need careful analysis and critical thinking to make the best of existing opportunities.

Your communication and people skills, naturally, are of critical importance, as a large part of your work will be done over the phone or email – both negotiating and closing deals. If you have – or can build up – some experience in the transportation industry in another role, this can be very beneficial for your brokering, as you'll be better connected with the main players in the field.

1.2. Partner with a Good Consultant or Trainer (www.MiltonCollier)

Besides the general skills you need to refresh or develop, you might want to partner with a good Freight Broker Consultant or Trainer to get fully prepared for actual requirements of the brokering job. Getting the top freight broker training books is also important, so you can always refer to them when you're unsure how to go ahead.

Investing in transportation broker training with an expert can give you deep insight into the workings of the industry and its main players. You'll also pick up practical knowledge about the work of a freight broker, and learn how to work with shippers, and how to handle shipping rates negotiations. Let's not forget that training can lead you to open freight broker jobs too, and potentially open many doors for your business.

2. Choose a Company Name and Register Your Business

In order to legally operate a brokerage, you will also have to choose a company name and register your business. Part of registering is also carefully selecting the kind of entity you'd like to register as – sole proprietor, partnership, Limited Liability Company or corporation – and then registering your business in your state at your local business license department.

3. Develop a Business Plan

Your business plan includes a go-to-strategy and the more you invest in figuring out the specifics and researching the market, the better you will be prepared to meet its challenges.

4. Find the Right Carriers

A freight broker without carriers is like a ship without sails. Part of your go-to-market strategy should also include finding the carriers which work in the field of operations you've chosen for yourself. What's more, the right carriers are also the ones that are trusted, reliable and professional. This makes the task hard but not impossible!

From online directories and direct references by other brokers to networking events, there is a multitude of ways to find the right carriers for yourself, so don't hesitate to try out a number of them and don't just go with what feels easiest!

5. Apply For a USDOT Number and Get Your Broker Authority

After you've gotten acquainted with the important role of the freight broker, and what you need to get started in terms of education and a business plan, it's time to delve into the legal side of how to become a freight broker.

Before you start operating in the field, you need to get a freight broker license from the Federal Motor Carrier Safety Administration (FMCSA). The licensing is also referred to as obtaining your Motor Carrier Operating Authority (MC authority).

Your first step in getting licensed is to get a USDOT number, which is required on the application form. Then you can start the registration process on FMCSA's website. Along with filling in the freight broker application form, OP-1, you have to also pay the one-time application fee of $300. You can find further instructions for filling in OP-1. The processing time is between four and six weeks.

Once your application has been approved, the FMCSA will send you your MC number by mail.

The MC number, however, does not mean you can start business yet. When it's issued, it gets posted on the Register page of the FMCSA. Within 10 days, anybody who finds a problem with your registration can protest against it. After this period, you are granted the MC authority.

6. Get a Freight Broker Bond

As just mentioned in the previous section, to get your MC authority from the FMCSA, you need to obtain a freight broker bond, or a BMC-84 bond. If you've been following the freight news, you're probably aware that back in 2013, the bond requirement was raised to $75,000 to ensure high industry standards and accountability.

If you've never worked with surety bonds before, it's important to understand what they are: in essence, a three-party contract. Your freight brokerage is the principal, the FMCSA is the oblige, and the surety is the one providing the bond.

The purpose of the freight broker bond is to guarantee that you will follow all applicable rules and regulations in your brokering. In this sense, the bond is an additional line of credit for your business. Because of the risk involved in providing you with this, when you apply for a bond, the surety needs to take a close and hard look at your personal and business finances, as well as your credit score and the overall stability of your business.

On the basis of this evaluation, the surety decides your bond premium, or your actual your freight broker bond cost. That's right: you don't need to pay the whole bonding amount, but only a percentage of it.

If your credit score is above 700, you're likely to pay between 1.25% to 3% premiums, or between $937 and $2250. For applicants with credit score between 650 and 699, the percentages are between 3.5% and 5%, or $2,625 and $3,750. Even if your credit is far from perfect, you can still get bonded with a bad credit program, though you'll have to pay slightly a higher premium to mitigate the risk involved.

In general, the best tip to reduce the price you have to pay for your freight broker bond is to work on improving your credit score. You can find more smart tips on reducing your costs when renewing your bond yearly in this useful freight broker bond renewal guide.

7. Obtain Contingent Cargo Insurance and General Liability

With your MC number you can go ahead with getting insurance (Form BMC-34 for loss and damage and in some cases, Form BMC-91 or BMC-91X for bodily injury, property damage and environmental restoration) and your surety bond, which we detailed in the previous section.

You need these insurances because many, if not most, shipping companies will request that you present these before you begin work together.

8. Designate Agents for Service of Process

At this stage, once you've obtained your bond and insurance, you're ready to choose your process agents for each state you do business in. This can be done through Form BOC-3 (Designation of Agents for Service of Process) which you need to fill in and submit to the FMCSA.

9. Get Your Operation Tools and Resources

When it comes to the material assets you need to start a brokerage, there are a few things to consider – even if you don't plan to open a physical office in the beginning.

The essential technical gear that you need at first includes a computer, a printer, a copy and fax machine, a landline phone and a mobile one, some office supplies – and a solid internet connection. You might also want to look into freight brokering software, as it can automate a part of your work and boost your productivity. With time, you'll see what other items or services are necessary and get them as the need arises, but these are the basics.

10. Get Enough Initial Operational Capital (Factoring Company)

Unless you have enough cash already at your disposal, you will probably have to consider a Factoring Company to pay your Carriers/Drivers. Since you will be the intermediary between shippers and carriers, you'll often have to pay truckers for the shipment before you've received the payment from the shipper.

11. Market Your Business

The final bit you need to cover is how you will market your brokerage to potential clients. Here you can think about what will make you stand out and how you can get your message across best.

From a marketing strategy and social media profiles with regular posts to a great website with a blog and printed marketing materials – the scope depends on what you think will impress future clients most.

Objectives

- o Upon successful completion of the Freight Broker/Freight Agent Training Program, you'll:

o Understand the process of freight brokering from start to finish

o Have the tools needed to be successful as a freight broker or freight agent

o Learn the basics of day-to-day operations of a brokerage or agency

o Use techniques such as prospecting, sales and marketing, rating, and negotiations

o Be able to manage a shipment from origin to destination

o Gain valuable industry resources

Details

Become a part of the exciting trucking, freight logistics, and transportation industries as a licensed freight broker or as a freight broker agent. From licensing to operations, to sales and marketing, you'll learn the basics of how to run a domestic freight brokerage or agency in the United States.

Entrepreneur magazine has rated the freight brokerage business as one of the top home-based businesses to own, and a recent Wall Street Journal article cited freight brokering and logistics as the largest growing sector of the transportation industry. Written by freight brokerage specialists, the Freight Broker/Agent Online Training Program will provide you with the knowledge and resources needed to break into the $400 billion-plus shipping industry.

Freight broker professionals are in demand. No matter the state of the economy, goods will always need to be shipped.

A motivated and disciplined freight broker or freight agent who has received the proper training can build up his or her business into a six-figure earning potential. It's an ideal home business for a self-starter who enjoys fast-paced work.

Freight Broker Basics

Overview of the Job

<u>In this training section you will learn:</u>

o What is a Freight Broker?

A freight broker is an individual or company that serves as a liaison between another individual or company that needs shipping services and an authorized motor carrier. Though a freight broker plays an important role in the movement of cargo, the broker doesn't function as a shipper or a carrier. Instead, a freight broker works to determine the needs of a shipper and connects that shipper with a carrier willing to transport the items at an acceptable price.

To operate as a freight broker, a business or individual must obtain a license from the Federal Motor Carrier Safety Administration (FMCSA). Freight brokers are also expected to carry insurance to protect both their business clients and their customers from loss. In many areas, freight brokers are required to carry surety bonds as well.

Freight broker services are valuable to both shippers and motor carriers. Freight brokers help shippers find reliable carriers that might otherwise be difficult to locate. They assist motor carriers in filling their trucks and earning money for transporting a wide variety of items. For their efforts, freight brokers earn commissions.

Freight brokers use their knowledge of the shipping industry and technological resources to help shippers and carriers accomplish their goals. Many companies find the services provided by freight brokers indispensable. In fact, some companies hire brokers to coordinate all of their shipping needs.

Often, freight brokers are confused with forwarders. Though a freight forwarder performs some of the same tasks as a freight broker, the two are not the same. A forwarder takes possession of the items being shipped, consolidates smaller shipments, and arranges for the transportation of the consolidated shipments. By contrast, a freight broker never takes possession of items being shipped.

Many freight brokers gain experience in the industry by working for a shipper or carrier. In this way, an aspiring broker can gain technical knowledge, as well as vital business contacts. Others enroll in freight broker training courses. However, such training courses can be costly and do not always provide the connections important for success in this field.

Some freight brokers begin their careers as agents rather than actual brokers. Freight broker agents are independent contractors who work as representatives of a broker. These agents handle assigned areas and are able to operate locally even without having numerous contacts in the industry. Startup costs for broker agents are usually minimal. Typically, a computer, telephone, and fax machine are all that is required to work as a home-based agent for a freight broker.

Take a look around your home or office. It's highly unlikely you have much--if anything at all--that didn't reach you either entirely or partially by truck. The size and scope of the motor freight industry is almost overwhelming. The good news is, there's still plenty of room for you to start and grow a profitable business serving the industry as a freight broker.

What exactly is a freight broker? Very simply, it's an individual or a company that brings together a shipper that needs to transport goods with an authorized motor carrier that wants to provide the service.

A freight broker falls into the category of transportation intermediary, which is a company that is neither a shipper nor an asset-owning carrier, but plays a role in the movement of cargo. "Transportation intermediaries leverage their knowledge, investment in technology and people resources to help both the shipper and carrier succeed," says Milton L. Collier.

Brokers provide an important and valuable service to both motor carriers and shippers. They help carriers fill the trucks and earn a commission for their efforts. They help shippers find reliable motor carriers that they (the shippers) might not have otherwise known about. In fact, some companies use brokers as their traffic department, allowing the broker to coordinate all their shipping needs.

Brokers aren't new to the trucking industry; they've been around since the industry itself began in the early part of the 20th century. Prior to the 1970s, however, regulations governing brokers were so restrictive that few firms were willing to even try to gain entry into the industry. But with dramatic changes in federal transportation policy during the 1970s, regulatory restrictions have eased, creating new entrepreneurial opportunities in the third-party logistics arena.

The Players

An industry so huge and diverse requires a wide range of participants to thrive. Some of these participants' titles may be a bit confusing, and some of their responsibilities may overlap. But to keep things as clear and simple as possible, let's look at who the key players are and what they do.

Freight broker. A freight broker is the middleman who connects shippers and carriers.

Shipper. A shipper is an individual or business that has products or goods to transport.

Motor carrier. A motor carrier is a company that provides truck transportation. There are two types of motor carriers: private (a company that provides truck transportation of its own cargo) and for hire (a company that is paid to provide truck transportation of cargo belonging to others).

The Different between a Freight Broker and Agent

With the fast-growing freight shipping industry, many logistic companies are hiring freight broker agents. There are companies offering on-the-job training and great work from home opportunities to freight brokerage agents with a strong customer-base. But, unfortunately many people are not aware of the fundamental difference between a freight broker and a freight broker agent.

Freight Broker

A freight broker is a self-sufficient person who must have authority to run his or her business. A completely self-employed broker can send invoices to customers on his or her own name. Freight brokers also pay to freight carriers. In short, they run their whole business independently.

Freight Broker Agent

Agents typically work for another broker and thus they need to have a broker authority. They endorse the authority of the brokers for whom they work. They aren't responsible for paying to freight carriers, trucks, and sending invoices to the customers. Freight broker agents charge broker a commission for their assistance or work.

How opportunities vary for brokers and agents

Agents have all the freedom in the world to expand their client-base, and that too without sticking their head into broker authority and invoicing. There are many agents who make a handsome salary every month and find no need of becoming a broker. An agent needs to keep a track on the market, so they don't miss on any major update that may impact on their business. They should also be capable of understanding all sorts of trucking and logistics solutions offered by the industry.

Unlike agents, freight brokers have more responsibilities imposed by the government of the respective nation. In the USA, brokers apply for authority through the FMCSA, which is an acronym of Federal Motor Carrier Safety Administration. FMCSA is managed by the US department of transportation. Brokers must have proper insurance and forms, which can be a tedious and time-consuming job if you're not well-acquainted with the freight shipping industry.

Agents usually work from their home independently, without a single employee. So, there is no one to compete with. And no register! The scenario is different for freight brokers. They need to collect payments from their clients and make payments to the trucks they used for freight shipping. If the broker has an agent or a team of agent, he or she needs to pay them as well; the amount is a commission which is determined by considering the gross line haul rate.

The agent calculates the line haul rate for the shipment, look for trucks, response to customer calls, and help the truck driver with the directions to the receiver for a broker he or she works for. But the trucking companies send invoices to the broker, not to the agent. As you can see, a broker has to do more of the administrative kind of work.

Typically, the agent works for a broker as an independent contractor. A committed work from home agent could earn more than $1500 a day. Cargo freight shipping has become one of the fastest growing industries today.

Why Shipper Use Freight Brokers?

You might wonder why shippers would need to use a freight broker to move their goods and what a freight broker is in general. Well, today we will answer those two very important questions for you.

Many businesses have limited resources and time to establish relationships with trucking carriers to move their product on a routine basis.

Therefore, they hire freight brokers. A freight broker is in constant communication with the trucking industry and has the expertise to negotiate competitive freight rates with the carriers all while taking in account the customer's requests.

A shipper's core concern is manufacturing a product and distributing it. The freight broker's core concern is moving those products from origin to destination and having it arrive to the customer in its desired condition. With the limited in-house resources it can get very expensive for the shipper as well as time consuming to handle all the necessary work of setting up shipments directly with carriers. Shippers must focus their attention on what matters most and that is their product and let the freight broker handle the shipping of that product.

Freight brokers use their sheer amount of volume done with carriers to benefit the customer directly by getting the most competitive freight rates upwards of 80% off. Many trucking companies do not have a sales staff and some of which just have one truck and driver so they must rely on a freight broker to keep their business going. This established relationship between the freight broker and carrier helps make it routine for both ends and keep things running as smoothly as possible.

In summary, a shipper uses a freight broker rather than attempting to set-up their shipment themselves due to the convenience, cost-effectiveness, and expertise in the field by the freight broker. They are geared to a commitment of excellence in customer service, from the initial shipping quote inquiry to the arrival of our customer's shipment at its final destination.

Asset of Non Asset Based Freight Broker

The Shipper will ask you, "Are you an asset based company"? Why some shippers require brokers to own assets? Could it be as simple as the shipper not entirely understanding the world of freight brokering? Perhaps, but rarely is anything that simple. Let's explore further some of the myths surrounding why a shipper would require assets and then prove once and for all why non asset based freight brokers can be a valuable ASSET to almost any shipper regardless of size.

Myth #1 Non Asset Based Freight Brokers Don't Have Direct Access to Trucks

It's often perceived if a freight broker is non-asset based that they don't have direct access to trucks. This couldn't be any further from the truth. Most freight brokers have access to thousands of trucks through various carrier partnerships. It may come as a big surprise to some shippers but, as a result of not being asset based, the freight broker's network of trucks is typically much larger and more flexible then even the largest asset based carriers. For example if a trucking company owns 50 trucks versus a broker that has 1,000 carriers averaging 6 trucks each it's obvious that the broker has more capacity to assist his customer in moving their freight because they are able to cast a wider net.

FACT: Experienced freight brokers can give shippers instant access to a large pool of qualified carriers and increased flexibility.

Myth #2 Non Asset Based Freight Broker Are Not Cost Effective

Some shippers believed that non asset based freight brokers can't be competitive when it comes to price. Their thought is, if you remove the broker from the transaction it will result in lower prices for the shipper. Although it may seem logical, it's not completely accurate. As we all know, there is power is in numbers. As a result of a freight broker's volume in a given lane, within a given market or with a group of carriers, they are able to leverage that volume and negotiate better pricing. Equally important is the fact that freight brokers routinely re-position assets resulting in less empty miles and more profit retention for their asset based carrier partners. Because no carrier wants to run empty, back hauls are typically done at a discounted rate which allows brokers to offer competitive rates while earning a small profit.

FACT: Smart freight brokers are able to leverage back hauls and volume to decrease their cost basis which allows them to make a small profit while maintaining competitive prices.

Myth #3 Non Asset Freight Brokers Have Less Control Than Asset Based

It's easy for a shipper to assume if a Broker doesn't own the assets that they in fact have no control. This too is inaccurate. Most freight brokers require their carriers to comply with strict company policies as it relates to compliance and performance. For example, experienced freight brokers require carriers to meet the highest safety standards as well as insuring all their carriers have an active carrier authority and are properly insured.

Smart brokers also monitor their carrier's service performance including on-time pickup, on-time delivery, complaints as well as freight claims.

If service falls below a certain level, carriers are many times deemed NO LOAD to prevent future issues. .

When it comes to loss and/or damage of a shipment, shippers are sometimes concerned that they will not be reimbursed for damages during transit. The fact is, broker are required by the FMCSA to perform due diligence on every carrier including making sure each motor carrier they use has both a valid authority as well as the proper insurance to cover the value of the freight onboard in the event of a claim. Believe it or not this due diligence requirement that broker are required to perform on every motor carrier they use is a major benefit to doing business with brokers that is typically over looked. Not to mention that when a carrier legally or illegally brokers a load, any claims filed as a result of that load will not typically be covered by the carrier's primary cargo insurance. In addition, good non asset based freight brokers carry at least $100,000 in contingent cargo insurance to help supplement the primary cargo insurance carried by asset based carrier.

FACT: Good brokers are masters at controlling the "controllable." When it comes to delays due to weather, traffic, driver illness and equipment breakdown carriers have no advantage whether a customer's product picks up or deliver on time in good condition.

So now what? We know that some shippers are reluctant to use non asset freight brokers. We've learned that a minority of shippers either don't have a clear understanding of how experienced freight brokers work and/or they have been misinformed, causing them to shy away from freight brokers without assets.

At the end of the day, freight brokers play a vital and growing role in the world of logistics and will continue to play a vital role into the foreseeable future. The good news is more and more shippers are using non asset based broker's year over year so the perception is changing. Once it becomes clear to the shipper, the role that freight broker's play and how freight brokers can benefit them, the perception will change and the freight broker will have greater opportunities to convert those few reluctant shippers into customers. It simply and comes down to education, expectation, execution and delivery. In soliciting a hesitant shipper, if you are able to achieve these four key components, you're heading in the right direction and should find greater success in converting those shippers who are reluctant to use non asset based freight brokers.

II. Industry Overview

In this training section you will learn:

Overview of the Transportation Industry

Brief History of Surface Transportation and Freight Brokering

The U.S. Logistics and Transportation Industry

The logistics and transportation industry in the United States is highly competitive. By investing in this sector, multinational firms position themselves to better facilitate the flow of goods throughout the world's largest consumer market. International and domestic companies in this industry benefit from a highly skilled workforce and relatively low costs and regulatory burdens.

Spending in the U.S. logistics and transportation industry totaled nearly $1.3 trillion in 2011, and averaged 8.5 percent of annual gross domestic product (GDP). Analysts expect industry investment to correlate with growth in the U.S. economy.

A highly integrated supply chain network in the United States links producers and consumers through multiple transportation modes, including air and express delivery services, freight rail, maritime transport, and truck transport.

To serve customers efficiently, multinational and domestic firms provide tailored logistics and transportation solutions that ensure coordinated goods movement from origin to end user through each supply chain network segment.

Industry Subsectors

Air and express delivery services (EDS): Firms offer expedited, time-sensitive, and end-to-end services for documents, small parcels, and high-value items. EDS firms also provide the export infrastructure for many exporters, particularly small and medium-sized businesses that cannot afford to operate their own supply chain.

Freight rail: High volumes of heavy cargo and products are transported long distances via the U.S. rail tracking network. Freight rail moves more than 70 percent of the nation's coal, 58 percent of its raw metal ores, and more than 30 percent of its grain. This subsector accounted for approximately one third of all U.S. exports.

Logistics services: This subsector includes inbound and outbound transportation management, fleet management, warehousing, materials handling, order fulfillment, logistics network design, inventory management, supply and demand planning, third-party logistics management, and other support services. Logistics services are involved at all levels in the planning and execution of the movement of goods.

Maritime: This subsector includes carriers, seaports, terminals, and labor involved in the movement of cargo and passengers by water.

Water transportation carries about 78 percent of U.S. exports by tonnage via U.S.- and foreign-flag carriers.

Trucking: Over-the-road transportation of cargo is provided by motor vehicles over short and medium distances. The American Trucking Associations reports that in 2011, trucks moved 9.2 billion tons of freight, or about 67 percent of all freight tonnage transported domestically. Motor carriers collected $604 billion in revenues, or about 81 percent of total revenue earned by all domestic transport modes.

The transportation industry is enormous, encompassing everything from container ships that transport goods from port to port all around the globe; from the rail and trucking networks that move those containers across states, countries, and continents to the airliners we use to fly to destinations near and far for work and pleasure, to the express shipping companies "for when it absolutely, positively has to be there overnight."

The industry encompasses all those businesses that move people or goods, by land, sea, or air, from one point to another. This is a big industry, employing millions: In addition to the package deliverer, and truck driver of the industry-there's a beehive of behind-the-scenes workers bustling to load containers, fuel airplanes, coordinate the logistics of thousands of railroad cars, and chart the best routes for truck drivers to take across America.

Virtually everything that surrounds us-including our clothes-comes from somewhere else. Your computer's components, manufactured in multiple countries, all had to be transported to the computer manufacturer, assembled, and then transported to a store or perhaps your front door. The newspaper you read this morning could not have been produced (think of the trucks delivering logs to the paper mill; think of the paper and ink being delivered to the printing press) or delivered without the transportation industry. And then there's passenger travel-the airlines, trains, boats, and buses that people use every day to get from place to place.

Transportation may not be sexy, but it pervades nearly every area of our lives. Without the transportation industry, economies, global and domestic, would disintegrate.

Opportunities in the industry can be classified geographically, as local, regional, national, or international. In many career paths, you'll need to pay your dues in a local job before moving up to a regional transportation outfit, and you'll have to work at a regional one before moving to a national one. And if you go into freight transportation, be aware that this sector has been consolidating, as companies seek to become global players by merging into giant, full-service transportation integrators, combining ships, trains, boats, and rail.

"JUST-IN-TIME" TECHNOLOGY
Just-in-time technology allows businesses to avoid inventory costs by procuring goods only when they're needed. Take PC manufacturers like Dell or Gateway, which promise rapid delivery. Rather than gathering all of the parts necessary to make a PC, assembling all those parts, and storing the PC in inventory-tying up money that could be used for other purposes before anyone's actually purchased the PC, and increasing costs due to inventory maintenance-just-in-time technology allows PC manufacturers to order PC components, have the components delivered, have the components assembled into a PC, and ship the PC to the customer in a matter of hours. The freight transportation industry has earned new relevance thanks to its implementation of just-in-time technology.

There are two sides of the transportation industry: companies that move goods (freight and shipping companies) and companies that move people (passenger transportation companies). The biggest of the shipping companies are the ones that integrate several types of transportation services to offer clients efficient door-to-door service, thanks to just-in-time technology and containers that allow goods to be transferred seamlessly from ships to railroads to trucks. (This is called "intermodal" transport.)

Here's how the two sides of the transportation industry look when broken down by the type of vehicle used:

PLANE
The biggest shipping players in this segment-FDX Corporation (FedEx), DHL, and UPS-integrate air transportation with other types of transportation.

SHIP
About three quarters of all maritime shipping is transoceanic, including tankers that mostly carry petroleum.

The biggest shipping companies are based outside the United States: Taiwan's Evergreen Marine, Japan's Nippon Yusen Kabushiki Kaisha, and Denmark's AP Møller-Mærsk move enormous numbers of containers. Although the federal government is revitalizing U.S. performance in this segment through the use of advanced technology, job opportunities are generally better at the foreign companies.

TRUCK AND BUS
The trucking industry carries 80 percent of all consumer goods. The biggest players in this segment are integrated-transportation parcel-delivery companies such as United Parcel Services (UPS), FDX Corporation, and DHL. The sector includes trucking companies like Schneider National and Yellow Roadway Corporation, as well as truck rental companies like Amerco (best known for its U-Haul trucks).

RAIL
Freight trains mainly carry coal, grain, and lumber. After a period of intense consolidation in this segment, the four leading companies are Burlington Northern Santa Fe, CSX, Norfolk Southern, and Union Pacific.

LOGISTICS
At the most basic level, the logistics sector of the transportation industry makes sure the trains run on time. Logistics professionals make sure people and freight get from place to place when they're supposed to-and that they don't hold up the next leg of the trip that's waiting on their arrival (e.g. that airline passengers changing planes at airline hubs arrive on time to catch their connecting flights, or that the ocean freight shipment arrives in port in time to be transferred to the railway that's going to move it across the country before the train is scheduled to depart). Most big transportation companies have significant logistics departments to oversee these matters, but there are a number of sizeable companies that don't own the ships and trucks and other means of transportation, but rather just handle the logistics details for the companies that do.

Examples of these kinds of companies include C.H. Robinson Worldwide and Expeditors International of Washington. Other companies that contract to handle logistics for transportation companies include Kuehne & Nagel International, Schneider Logistics, and DHL Worldwide. Other players in this sector also include warehousing companies, such as Preferred Freezer Services, which provide warehousing services for transportation companies.

This is an industry that employs some 10 million people in the United States. If you want to hop aboard, however, you'll want to keep some things in mind.

Be aware that for many positions, you'll need to join a union-and in recent years, strikes and other labor disputes have been a part of life in the industry (just ask UPS, Northwest, American Airlines, and workers and management at U.S. ports). Old-line airlines, in particular, have been putting downward pressure on jobs as they try to fend off or emerge from bankruptcy.

Logistics, which involves planning and managing efficient transportation for everything from individual shipments (such as a book from your favorite e-commerce site) to entire fleets of trucks or planes (think: planning when and where the planes in FedEx's fleet will take off and land), has been growing in recent years as information technology advances have swept the industry. Today, it's possible to track shipments by satellite and thus improve the efficiency of the transportation and shipment process, and ongoing advances in technology should make this an area of strong job growth.

SMELLS LIKE TEAM SPIRIT

As in many other industries, the network of coworkers you develop in transportation will not only be important for your success, it'll be what makes the work fun. But transportation differs from some other industries in that there's very little snobbishness among the people in it. An insider says, "We help each other, wherever we are. This makes work easier and more enjoyable."

THE POWER OF TECHNOLOGY

Technology has changed the face of the transportation industry. If you're in logistics, for instance, expect to work with 3-D graphics or special software to help you arrange the placement of billions of tons of freight onboard a ship, or plan global shipping routes, or monitor shipments by satellite. An insider describes the innovative technology as "awesome," adding, "There are so many cutting-edge tools being developed every day to enhance tracking performance that it's a great challenge to be working with them."

III. Broker Laws and Requirements by the FMCSA

In this training section you will learn:

Legalities of Broker/Brokerage Services

Non-brokerage Services

Because freight brokers have to answer for shipments that cross state lines, your business will be overseen by federal authorities, particularly the Federal Motor Carrier Safety Administration under the 49 CFR §371 rule. In freight broker training school, you'll have a chance to study in detail all the rules that deal with freight brokering.

You already know the basic requirements for freight brokers – an operating license from the FMCSA, the services of process agents, and a surety bond for possible financial liabilities. Here's a quick summary of the other rules that govern freight brokering:

1. Working with Authorized Motor Carriers

A property or freight broker is part of the transportation industry so they go under the oversight of the Department of Transportation. Since you'll be working closely with motor carriers (or truckers), you'll have to register with the DOT using your FMCSA freight broker license.

Make sure that you only work with recognized entities to avoid risk or liability. That is, the motor carrier moving your load must carry an authority that matches yours. For example, if you have a property broker license, then you can only transact loads with a carrier that has a valid property motor carrier authority. If you arrange a load with a carrier that doesn't have the right license, say a household goods motor carrier authority against your property broker license, the FMCSA may subject you to penalties and fines. Frequent violations may lead to a cancellation of your freight brokering license altogether.

2. Record-Keeping

Liabilities are an unfortunate part of brokering that's why freight brokers need to maintain a record of each transaction for future reference. You'll be dealing with the same motor carriers and shippers most of the time so to simplify this task and eliminate unwieldy records-keeping, you can create a master list of these records. The following are the information that FMCSA must see in each transaction/master list of transactions:

Shipper's name and address

Carrier's name, address, and registration/USDOT number

Bill of lading/freight bill number

Freight brokering rates and the person who paid for the brokering service

Other non-brokerage services you did with regards to the shipment, how much you were paid for it, and the person who settled the obligation

Freight charges you collected and the date the motor carrier was paid for the shipment

There's no cut-and-dried rule on how to sort out this information. You can create a record tracker that fits your work flow as long as you capture all these data correctly.

Both your shippers and carriers have legal access to those transaction records that pertain to brokering services you did with or for them, up to a period of 3 years. After the third year, you can destroy these records.

3. Freight Broker Accounting

You may have other businesses alongside your freight brokerage. When it comes to revenues and expenses, the law requires separate financial records for your brokering firm. In case your businesses share common expenses—say rental and utilities—third parties must be able to identify what outlays are from the brokerage and what are not. Of course, it goes without saying that you must be able to explain how and why you assigned these amounts to the brokerage in an audit.

4. Misrepresentation

Whatever advertising that you do—whether in print, radio or web—your business must be what you say it is. That is, you cannot go around introducing yourself as a carrier to your customers if you are not. You have to use the same name which was approved in your freight broker license in any transaction that you do. Misleading information on your broker status can be a cause for liabilities or heavier penalties.

5. Double Brokering and Co-Brokering

Due diligence is required of all freight brokers, mainly because heavy penalties and liabilities could arise from unethical brokering practices. Two common industry practices—double brokering and co-brokering—present some problems.

Co-brokering is when you work with another freight brokerage in arranging transportation for a load that you can't handle anymore. This is legal and acceptable, as long as the agreement with the shipper allows for this arrangement.

Double brokering, on the other hand, is when a motor carrier contracts another carrier to handle a load you have given the first trucker. This practice is frowned upon and fraught with risks, particularly when shipment problems happen.

Whether you are aware of the double brokering or not, you may still have to pay the shipper for losses incurred related to the load. Authorities will examine due diligence steps you've taken to determine whether you're answerable for this error or not.

6. Brokering Exempt and Non-Exempt Commodities

When you arrange transportation for loads from shippers, you must be aware of the following rules governing exempt and non-exempt commodities:

List of items that are exempt from USDOT regulation, list of non-exempt items that are similar to exempt cargo or created from exempt cargo and freight not exempt under as stated.

You can always arrange shipments that contain unregulated freight. Shipments that have non-exempt cargo bring you under FMCSA oversight. Keep in mind that specific commodities require specific authorities for both freight brokers and motor carriers. The long and short of it:

If a shipment is exempt, then you don't need authority to broker the load nor does it need to be moved by an authorized carrier; and

If the load is non-exempt, then both you and the carrier need the appropriate authority to handle the cargo.

Failure to comply with exempt/non-exempt guidelines could be grounds for penalties, the suspension of your operating license, or worse, revocation of your freight broker license.

Double Brokering: For many years, the transportation industry has confounded "double brokering" and "co-brokering" to mean the same. Consequently, both have acquired a negative aura. It is important for the industry to understand the difference between double brokering and co-brokering, because one can be an asset to your brokerage business, while the other is a definite risk.

People often ask whether it is legal for a licensed transportation property broker to accept a load from its customer and give that load to another broker for assistance arranging transportation. The answer is yes, and it is known as co-brokering.

Not only is co-brokering legal, it may be advantageous at times to have another broker help cover a load, as long as the contract that the original broker has with its customer does not specifically prohibit co-brokering. When done properly, there is absolutely nothing wrong with co-brokering, assuming the transaction is handled in accordance with the permission of the original broker.

Downside of Double Brokering

There really are no benefits to double brokering - only risks. By the inherent nature of the transaction, double brokering is not the same as co-brokering.

When a motor carrier agrees to transport freight for a broker (under the guise it will haul the freight), and the carrier subsequently re-brokers it to another carrier, the freight has now been double brokered.

The same is true when a carrier (that also has broker authority) accepts a brokered load (as the carrier) and then tenders that load to another carrier through its brokerage (without the broker's knowledge or consent).

In either event, the original broker is now in a compromising situation:
It does not know who is actually handling the freight.

It does not know whether the actual carrier has the required permits.

It does not know if the carrier's insurance is adequate to protect the parties.

 It does not know what due diligence was performed to qualify the carrier.

Tracing the freight also becomes dubious at best, usually leaving the original broker with incorrect information to transmit to its customer.

The original broker also runs the risk of being caught in a potential double jeopardy situation. For example, if it pays the contracted carrier (that double brokered the load), and that carrier does not pay the actual carrier, the original broker (or its customer) may be held accountable to pay a second time for the same freight movement.

Undoubtedly, this type of substandard activity has aided in giving the transportation brokerage community a questionable reputation.

Benefits of Co-Brokering

Co-brokering is when a broker works with another broker to service a specific need, with all parties aware of each other's functions and responsibilities. The question at hand is not whether to deal with another broker, but rather to use another broker's resources to your advantage when your resources do not suffice.

The most important benefit of co-brokering is servicing your customer. It proves your brokerage has the available resources to service all their requests.

Beyond that, co-brokering can result in a profit on a transaction that your brokerage might have otherwise refused. After all, you're in business to do business, not refuse business. If you don't service your customer, someone else will.

Some brokers have developed niches that other brokers can use to their advantage in better servicing their customers. Some of the niches include border crossings, bonded freight, working with hazardous materials, oversize equipment and local contracts.

A broker's services are not limited by assets, but rather by its imagination to adapt and adjust to situations. Therefore, its abilities can be enhanced by leveraging the capabilities of other brokers. When brokers work together, it is usually because one has capabilities to complete whatever the other currently lacks. The bottom line is that co-brokering gives brokers the ability to adapt and adjust to unfamiliar situations.

By working together in a co-broker relationship, both brokers benefit, as well as the initial customer. All parties involved should have the satisfaction of a job well done by servicing a customer and maintaining a profit. The alternative would be to leave the money on the table for the competition to take.

An alliance with another broker is simply another opportunity to offer services that your brokerage did not have before the alliance. Once a broker recognizes the benefits of co-brokering (and decides to deal with other brokers), the broker can add the services of its co-brokering allies to its own portfolio, thereby widening its range of services offered. When it comes to liability and the bottom line, would you rather deal with a broker you know or a carrier you do not?

Before conducting business with another broker, you should perform adequate due diligence to research and get to know the company you are considering. This is a very important step that should not be discounted. There are contracts designed specifically for co-brokering, outlining what each party to the transaction can expect of the other.

Rebating and Compensation

(a) A broker shall not charge or receive compensation from a motor carrier for brokerage service where:

(1) The broker owns or has a material beneficial interest in the shipment or

(2) The broker is able to exercise control over the shipment because the broker owns the shipper, the shipper owns the broker, or there is common ownership of the two.

(b) A broker shall not give or offer to give anything of value to any shipper, consignor or consignee (or their officers or employees) except inexpensive advertising items given for promotional purposes.

Duties

A broker shall exercise responsible supervision and control over the customs business that it conducts

IV. Marketing and Sales

In this training section you will learn:

Market Niches

Market Trends

Competition

Networking

Promotions

Your Marketing Dollars

Choosing a Niche

There are many valid reasons for choosing a well-defined market niche.

By targeting a specific market segment, you can tailor your service package and marketing efforts to meet that segment's needs. You'll also develop a reputation for expertise that attracts new customers.

You can design your niche based on geography (either the location of the shippers or the destination of the freight), types of cargo (agricultural, perishable, oversized, bulk commodities, etc.), and size of loads, specific industries or some other special shipping need.

To choose a niche, first consider what types of shipments and/or shippers you'd enjoy working with.

You may opt to simply handle general commodity freight-materials that are typically easy to handle and don't require any special attention. Or you may want to develop some expertise in areas such as heavy equipment, oversized loads, perishable commodities or even hazardous materials.

Don't limit your specialization plan to the commonly accepted areas; instead, find your own niche. Bill T., for example, does some interesting work for retailers. One major national chain hires his company to handle the distribution of point-of-sale promotion displays that have to be delivered to hundreds of stores on the same day. Other big businesses use Bill's company to manage shipments related to store openings and closings.

Your next step is to conduct market research to determine if there's a sufficient demand for the services you want to provide. If there is, move ahead with your marketing plan. If there isn't, consider how you might adjust your niche to one that generates adequate revenue.

Just about everything must move at least part of the way to its final destination by truck. With that in mind, it's safe to say that almost every company is a potential customer for you. But if you take that approach, you'll have a tough time coming up with an effective, not to mention affordable, marketing plan.

What's wrong with just going after anybody in the world who might ever have to ship something by truck for any reason? Because that market segment includes literally millions of companies and individuals, and it's impossible for any small business to communicate effectively with a market that size. Can you afford to send even one piece of direct mail to 1 million prospective customers? Of course not. But when you narrow that market down to, for example, 500 or 1,000 customers in a particular area, doing a successful direct-mail campaign is much more affordable and manageable.

Keep these questions in mind as you form your marketing plan:

Who are your potential customers?

How many of them are there?

Where are they located?

How do they currently transport freight?

Can you offer them anything they aren't getting now?

How can you persuade them to do business with you?

Exactly what services do you offer?

Features and Benefits

Managing Objections

Personality Types

Building Trust

Sales Process and Growth

Generally, the best way to get customers is through the Internet and then getting on the phone.

So, your first contact will be over the phone - but on many occasions, you will be directed to voice mail. So what do you do? How do you handle this?

If you get a recording, listen carefully to get the shipping manager's name. He may say something like "Hi, this is Robert in shipping. Leave a message".

You may leave a message if you like; but in reality, the potential customer will not return the call. They are busy. So, you will call back again. If you can't get a live person after 3, 4 or 5 calls, you may want to leave a message. Again, they may not return the call.

So, you go on to the next person on your calling list.

If you get a live person when you call, you want to simply ask, "Do you use freight brokers?" This way you can get to the point without wasting everybody's time. If they don't, you move on. If they do, you will ask if they have a few minutes to talk. If so, you will start asking questions about their business.

Trust me, this is where you will separate yourself from those who don't know what they are doing. Many freight brokers don't have experience and they don't get properly training. They have no idea what to ask. You don't want to be in that broker's shoes because you will probably get the shake off.

Shippers want to talk to people who know what they are talking about.

There is much more to this but this is a general outline and may get you to thinking about how you are going to approach your potential customers. Don't blow it. Either get experience or get trained.

Prospecting – Getting Customers

As a Freight Broker / Agent is 90% prospecting. If you have no one to prospect then you have no work. Let start with Getting Customers:

Getting Customers Using a few of the Lead Generation Tools and Resources below:

123Loadboard.com - Access to Thousands of Potential Customers

Step 1: Click on Tools - Step 2: Click on Search Directory

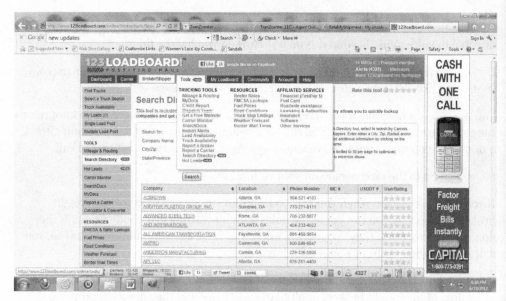

Prospecting – Getting Customers

Manta.com - Access to Over 60 Million of Potential Customers

Step 1: Register for FREE

Step 2: Search Company Type (Over 29 Millions)

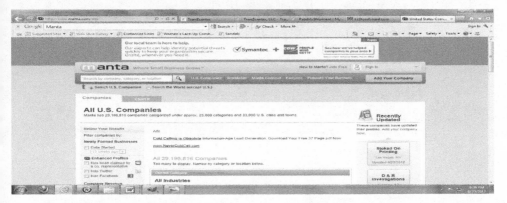

Prospecting – Getting Customers

Step 3: Results from Search (Furniture)

Step 4: Contact Information from Search

Prospecting – Getting Customers

Thomasnet.com - Access to Millions of Potential Customers

Step 1: Register for FREE

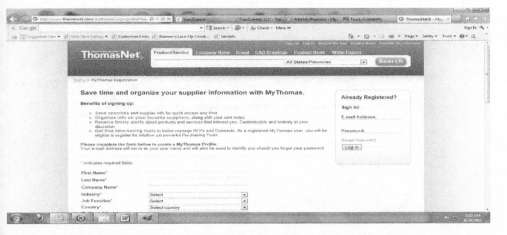

Step 2: Search Company Type

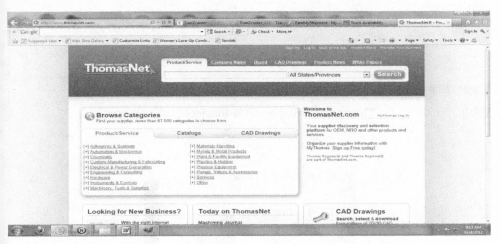

Prospecting – Getting Customers

Step 3: Result from Search

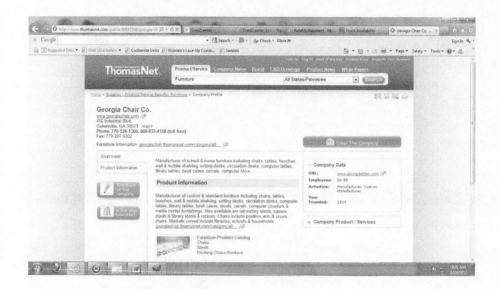

Prospecting – Getting Customers

UShip.com: Access to Thousands of Shippers/Customers (Bidding System)

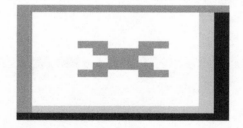

Prospecting

This is your starter list. It will provide you work as soon as you are able to broker.
While you are waiting for your authority to become active, or in the process of obtaining
a broker/agent contract, you can get a jump by starting your list now. Again, I remind

you, that you should not attempt to set-up customers without your active authority or a broker/agent contract in place.

You can; however, get the preliminary work of find contact names and numbers as well as doing tasks that allow you to fill your prospect list.

The number one reason freight brokers fail is complacency. They come out of the chute with high hopes, great expectations, and enthusiasm (which they should). They start by doing everything they were trained to do and begin to make money. They find themselves quickly obtaining every goal that they have set for themselves. Then, something happens, they become complacent. They begin to neglect their prospecting. Instead of prospecting today, they might play a round of golf, go to the mall with a friend, or go fishing. It doesn't matter what it is that they do, what matters is what they aren't doing, PROSPECTING!

Being a freight broker is a business of relationships. These relationships can change overnight. For instance, let's say Bill (our hypothetical freight broker), who has slacked on his prospecting, calls his shipper at ABC Manufacturing. He dials the direct line to Dave. Davis is the traffic manager at ABC that Bill has been dealing with for the last several months. It's taken a while but Dave and Bill have a solid relationship. Bill knows that he'll move $5000.00 worth of ABC's freight this week and every week because of their relationship. From this one account Bill earns from $500.00 to $750.00 every week. Today is different!

Dave got promoted, transferred, quit or worse, ABC had been sold and the home office in Omaha will handle all shipping. Whatever the reason, Dave isn't there anymore. The person that has taken Dave's place is an experienced traffic manager that has just come aboard from XYZ Company, and has his own brokers which he has relationships with.

Overnight, Bill lost $500.00 - $750.00 worth of weekly income with nothing to replace it because he quite or slacked on his prospecting. He assumed he would always have Dave and ABC. He assumed wrong and now has to eat the loss rather than having an account or accounts in place to help absorb the loss so that Bill's lifestyle can continue as normal.

Prospecting

Obtaining an account is rather quick and easy. The ability to build a relationship with an account, so that you become your shippers' favorite broker, is what takes time. More often than not, when you obtain an account, you will be offered the everyday loads which are offered to everyone. Build a relationship and you will find your shipper calling you and giving you the loads that aren't on the list. The cherry loads, so to speak.

They are the loads that don't need to be on a list because your shipper knows that they are easy to move and in high demand. The shipper knows that all they need to do is make one phone call and the load will be taken care of. You should strive to build your relationship with the shipper so that you are the phone call he makes in order to move the load.

This takes time. This is why you need to allow yourself at least 3 months to start seeing a regular paycheck. It's not getting the accounts, but rather the building of relationships that takes time. Think back to a time when you were single. Getting a date wasn't that hard. With that said how long did you and your spouse date before getting married? 6 months? A year? Longer? Although you're not going to marry your shipper, (although I have seen it happen), you're still building a relationship, and this takes time.

As you start to prepare your prospect list, keep this in mind. The worst part of beginning a career as a freight broker is the initial prospecting. After you begin your business and become established you will still need to prospect but it becomes easier.

The first part of creating your prospect list is self-explanatory. You're writing down companies in your area that you know are there. These are gimme's (southern for "give me").

Your friends and family that work for companies that use trucks to transport their product are a bit different. You can write these down and start calling them now. The purpose of the call is not to set them up as a customer, but to find out who is the "decision maker". The traffic manager, shipping clerk, head dispatcher or whatever their title may be. Every company has their own title for the person responsible for shipping. Your friends and family that are truck drivers may be contacted now as well. What you want from them are the names and numbers of as many shippers and receivers where they have loaded or delivered that you can get. You want their input on which companies they liked to pick-up at or deliver to and the one's they didn't. If possible you want to find out which loads they hauled that were brokered. Not all companies use brokers, so if you're able to find out from your truck driver the companies that did, you're a step ahead.

Prospecting

There is no minimum or maximum number of prospects that should be on your list. Just keep in mind that you can never quit prospecting. You should start getting in the habit of looking for prospects no matter where you are or what you are doing. Are you on a weekend outing? See a business that you suspect use trucks? Write them down or make mental note, as they should be added to your prospect list. Reading the paper and see a new company coming to your area? Add them to your list.

As you begin to broker you will have drivers call you. As you talk to drivers, listen. Keep in mind that most drivers are in their truck alone with little to no human contact. When they have a chance to talk to a live person, they talk. With a little conversation leading on your part, you can learn details of the last several loads they have picked-up and delivered.

What is conversation leading? The art of having a conversation with a person while leading the conversation to what you want to discuss with or without their knowledge.

Think back to the last time you were with a salesperson. Replay the conversation in your mind. If you had a good salesperson you'll find that the conversation was led by the salesperson, not you.

You may have been asking the questions, but the experienced salesperson would have answered your question in a way that led you to your next question or statement. This question or statement would not have been as spur of the moment by you as you might think. The sales person knew that his answer would cause you to have a certain response, be it in the form of a question or statement. He was able to achieve the desired outcome by leading the conversation. A skilled sales person, using this technique can essentially have you sell yourself through a series of planned questions. Drivers will sometimes call you about loads and to be dispatched by you on a load his company scheduled through you. To lead this conversation you could follow the example below:

> You: Where are you coming from?
>
> Driver: ST. Louis
>
> You: Load of beer?
>
> Driver: No, picked up motor oil.
>
> You: Cool, we ship motor oil out there all the time. You pick up at Smitty's?
>
> Driver: No, I picked up at Global.

Prospecting

Another form of prospecting that you will be able to employ once you begin is through you own shipper. You're set-up with ABC Manufacturing in Your Town, USA. You Google's ABC and found that they have distribution facilities all over the country. Since you're already set-up with ABC you have an instant in with the other facilities. You're already part of the team.

You may even call your contact at ABC and see if they know the contacts at6 the other facilities. If they do, you have names. Let your shipper know what you're doing so if they get a call from one of the other facilities they won't be blind-sided, and know to give you a glowing recommendation.

Another way to prospect is to call your customers' customer. This holds true especially if your shipper is a supplier. Perhaps you have a shipper that supplies gadgets to another manufacturer so that they can product their product. If so, then your customers' customer is a shipper too, this makes them a prospect. Again it is advised that you inform your shipper of what you are doing in advance.

When prospecting, use your imagination. We had a gentleman attend a FBT Workshop that owned an insurance company in Georgia. He wanted to add to his portfolio of businesses which he owned but also wanted new prospects for his insurance company. He wanted to grow his commercial underwriting business.

Talk about creative prospecting....His freight brokerage would not only earn him another form of revenue, in the process he would be collecting names, numbers and contacts of carriers, shippers and receivers, in which he would use as prospects for his insurance company. Never quit prospecting.

As you gain experience as a freight broker you will find other ways to prospect. Keep an open mind as the list is endless.

Another gimme is that you will know what kind of freight your prospect ships before you make your initial call. By knowing the freight they ship you will know, or at least have an idea, the kind of eq1uipment they will need.

VI. Overcoming Challenges

There are a multitude of details and procedures that freight brokers follow. These procedures and details involve a great deal of coordination with both the shipper and the carrier.

Here are 7 tips that will help you manage and coordinate your freight broker duties.

1. Understand the needs and desires of both shippers and motor carriers.
One of the biggest items of importance for shippers is "cost". Big companies employ entire logistics departments to find the most cost-effective route and method to move their cargo. Some large shippers use their own trucks; some use freight brokers; and some allow their customer to arrange for the transportation. Smaller shippers rely more upon freight brokers to move their cargo. But both large and small shippers have "cost" at the top, or close to the top, of their priorities.

Carriers also place a priority on "cost". The current situation with high fuel costs and other high operating expenses have taken a toll on the availability of trucks. This availability, commonly known as "capacity", has been dwindling for several years.

While shipper rates have increased, it's unlikely that rates have kept pace with a trucker's ongoing costs. The bottom line is, the truck needs to cover not only the actual costs but he or she needs to generate a profit on top of the costs.

2. Understand that the freight broker needs to negotiate a win-win-win situation whereby everyone achieves their goals - shipper, carrier and freight broker. Negotiating skills come easy for some people; others hate the idea of "haggling" with opposing parties. A good negotiator will understand that there is, at times, a "give-and-take". Knowing when to "hold em" and when to "fold em" can result in huge profits over time. The best way to exercise this "hold em and fold em" tactic will come from a broker monitoring his or her profit margin along with other important items such as volume of loads and days-in-collection on the receivables from shippers.

3. Pay attention to sound business fundamentals.
There are many successful freight brokers. Some have been around for quite a while; others are just getting a good start. Of these successful brokers, each and every one, most likely, has relied upon sound business fundamentals. In fact, that's probably the very reason for their success. It takes more than just "brokering" to be successful. It takes a person to "purpose" to pay attention to marketing, cash management, planning and creating an operating blueprint.

Each of these four topics has had volumes written about them. Without attention to these, a freight broker is most likely doomed to failure - regardless of his or her brokering knowledge.

4. On finding shippers, find a strategy that works and then stick with it - but keep experimenting as well.
One of the biggest fears for beginning freight brokers is how and where to find shippers. It's not as difficult to find shippers as one might think. However, it is difficult to find good paying shippers who also have loads that are relatively easy to cover.

One of the most effective (but not easy) methods is to search the internet using unique keywords. There are plenty of various shipper directories available; but then you've got thousands of other brokers calling the same shippers as you are.

Unique keyword searches will likely uncover shippers who aren't being called by every freight broker in the country.

5. When a shipper wants a quote or your rates, find out more about what you can expect. Some shippers will require quotes before they accept your set up package. Some of their

requests will involve 10, 15, 20 or more loads. Others will want a quote on just a specific load.

Sometimes the shipper is using you to gather information on how to price his load.

Other times the shipper will throw your quote into a large pool of other quotes - and there it stays with the shipper having no intention of actually giving you the load.

Here's what to do: Ask the shipper how often a particular load or loads are available. Are they daily, weekly, monthly? Make sure you understand if the shipper needs a dry van, reefer, flatbed or whatever. Refer to various pricing sources that provide the "going rates" for various lanes. If the shipper responds after you have given a quote that the quote is too high, tell the shipper that you'd like to try to cover the load for what he or she wants to pay. And ask for the order.

6. Get set up with as many carriers as you can regardless of whether or not you have a load for them.
There may be many, many incoming phone calls in response to some loads you have posted on the internet. Many of these calls will be "dead end" calls as the carrier is looking for either a higher rate or whatever.

However, while talking to the carrier, get him or her talking about what THEY are looking for in regards to what lanes they like, how many and what kinds of trucks they have, etc. If you "hit it off" with them, ask them if you can get set up with them. Most likely they'll say yes. Then you have one more carrier in your database.

7. Be prepared for things to go awry at times.
In addition to "dotting your I's and crossing your T's", be not only mentally prepared for problems - have some specific plans in place.

For example, let's say you think you have a load covered. The carrier has said, "Yes, I want the load". And you've sent out your set-up package, you've received the broker-carrier agreement back. Next you prepare and fax out the carrier confirmation. However, it doesn't come back and your phone calls go unanswered. So what do you do? You first consider yourself "dropped".

However, you will probably be getting phone calls after you think you have a load covered. So what do you tell them?

You tell them that you "think" you already have the load covered but you ask them to leave their name and call back number just in case something falls through.

This, sometimes, is a lifesaver when things do fall through.

VII. Success and the Broker/Agent

In this training section you will learn:

What is a Freight Broker? Why Become a Broker or Agent?

Benefits and Opportunities

Traits of a Successful Broker/Agent

Goal Setting

Developing a Plan

Qualities of Success

8 Traits Successful Freight Brokers Have in Common

Freight brokers live a fast-paced life, in an informal round table discussion with active and successful freight brokers and agents, we were able to dig out the top eight traits that most of them (and their peers) shared, listed here in random order:

1. They are self-motivated.

The successful freight broker is driven by passion, a reason for being if you like. Whether it's more time with the family, enough resources to support a hobby, or whatever it is that drives your enthusiasm, this motivation is the key that kicks them off the bed early in the morning and gets them going throughout a hectic workday.

You'd be surprised: money isn't often the top motivator for successful freight brokers. The reason they give why money takes second, third or even fourth place to a burning passion? When the business is slow and the cash register's not ringing much, this "reason for being" helps them slog through the rough patch.

2. Successful brokers have a strategic mindset.

Much of the daily routine of a freight brokerage involves a thousand and one details. When you're embroiled in these for too long, there's the tendency to not see the forest for the trees. You lose sight of the Big Picture—your vision for setting up a freight brokerage business. You start making decisions that's long on short-term advantages but short on long-term benefits. When that happens, your business could quickly lose its competitive advantage and stop getting better.

Successful freight brokers with a strategic mindset continually review and refine how they do things, unafraid to learn new things. They're also aware of what's going on in their industry, particularly with their competitors and partners, so that their business can easily and quickly adapt to any negative (or even positive) market changes.

3. They are results driven.

Successful freight brokers can set goals and define the tactical actions to obtain the results they want.

Some business owners often get trapped in the launch preparations of a new venture—crafting the business plan, studying the market, perfecting documentations and procedures and a million other details. Often, the thing that could spell success is the ability to hit the ground running even if all your ducks aren't in a row yet.

You can always refine and redefine as you go as long as you're doing something tangible and measurable to achieve the goals you have set for yourself and your brokering firm. Other freight brokers have found that setting benchmarks and milestones towards achieving an objective help them chop up a big goal into small, manageable, and achievable pieces.

4. They are highly customer oriented.

The freight brokerage sector has a customer-centric culture. A happy customer is a repeat (and loyal) customer. Successful brokers are helpful and devoted to the customer's interest to keep the business flourishing. In this case, the shippers' interest on the speedy and safe delivery of their shipments and the carriers' focus on getting paid decently and on time.

Freight brokers who have a deep base of repeat customers are anticipatory and responsive to the needs of the public they serve. It's not "what's in it for me?" but "what can I do to help?" that keeps their business continually viable.

5. The best have a proactive perspective.

When loads are moving from shipper to consignee, many things are going on at the same time. Many things can also go wrong. Anticipating problem areas and having different response mechanisms to address things that could go wrong is the mark of a successful freight broker. You must know what to do when a truck breaks down in the middle of a desert highway or an accident happens. Successful freight brokers don't only have a Plan B in place; they also have a Plan C (or even a Plan D) just in case.

6. They're very decisive.

When you have the big picture firmly in mind, choosing what to do first among what's necessary, urgent or important cuts your decision-making time in half. Knowing which tasks to prioritize and which to put on the back burner when crunch time comes are useful skills in this profession. Successful freight brokers know what must be done first—and quickly.

7. Freight brokers nurture relationships.

Building and nurturing relationships for the long term is vital to growing a robust freight brokerage business. At the heart of your engagements is (1) the ability to cooperate with a diverse mix of individuals and organizations with an equally diverse culture and values; and (2) the communication savvy to maintain helpful, beneficial and harmonious relationships.

8. They're very flexible.

In this fast-paced environment, the successful broker has a firm handle on everything that's going on while doing other things at the same time. Multitasking is a skill that most think they have in spades but only a few has actually mastered. Make sure that you're multitasking smartly—that is, you're working on your strengths, not on your weaknesses.

Making it to the freight brokerage big leagues doesn't only mean knowing the theoretical stuff that you learn in freight broker training. Like these characteristic traits of successful freight brokers show, making it big means having a firm handle of the intangibles, too.

One of the most common questions I get from freight brokers is "How much can a freight broker make?" My answer is almost always the same, "It depends."

Generally Freight Brokers can make very good money. I have seen many make hundreds of thousands a year, but I've also seen a few make next to nothing. The wonder of the profession is that there is no cap on what a person can make. You are only limited by the amount of business you can do. Therefore if a person is dedicated, hardworking, and skilled in business and as a salesperson they can make much more money than many other professions could provide.

From my experience I would venture to guess that the average established Broker makes between $100,000 and $150,000 a year. That's not bad for a profession requiring no college degree, certifications, or state exams. Among startup opportunities out there it is also one of the most affordable. A brokerage requires very few costs for startup.

So how does a freight broker make all this money? It's pretty simple, really.

When a company wishes to move a load of freight from one point to the other, he will pay for it to be moved. When a shipper uses a broker, he pays the broker to move the freight, only the broker does not actually move the freight, but rather possesses the contacts and resources to find the right person to do the job. The broker turns around and pays a carrier a lower price to move the freight than what the shipping company paid the broker. This difference is called a "spread" and is the broker's margin or profit once operating expenses are paid for.

So if you charge a company $2,000 to move a load, and pay a carrier $1,850, you will retain a margin of $150. Each load will vary, but the current industry average spread per load is probably somewhere around this figure. Now is the most important factor that decides how much a broker makes. How many loads can you move per week? Most getting started out will move about 1-5 loads per week, once established you might move something like 5-10 or more loads each week. You will see that your annual income as a Freight Broker, then will vary directly by the number of loads you move.

For example, if a person moves an average of 5 loads per week at $150, it will amount to about $39,000 each year. If you move an average of 10 loads per week at the same margin, you'll be making around $78,000 per year. It obviously would continue up from there.

One thing to keep in mind is that no one ever moved a load without knowing how to and being familiar with the transportation industry. If you hope to be successful as a freight broker you will need either experience in the transportation industry, an education in freight brokerage, or preferably both.

VIII. Getting Started
In this training section you will learn:

Your Business Name

Setting Up Your Business

Filing for Your Broker Operating Authority

Filing for Your Surety Bond

Obtaining Your Process Agents

Freight shipping plays a vital role in business. Almost all products sold in stores are shipped there, and manufacturing plants rely on shipping to receive materials and distribute finished products. Freight brokerage businesses assist the shipping industry by establishing connections between shippers and freight companies. Freight brokerage businesses are licensed as property brokers by the Federal Motor Carrier Safety Administration, which is part of the U.S. Department of Transportation.

USDOT Number

Before you can start a freight brokerage business you must first apply for a USDOT number with the Department of Transportation. Though not specifically required to become a freight broker, the USDOT number is required when filling out the application to become a broker through the FMCSA.

Broker Authority

Broker authority is a license provided by the FMCSA authorizing individuals or companies to act as freight brokers. Broker authority is applied for by filling out MFCSA form OP-1 and selecting the "broker of property" option. Form OP-1 requires individual or company contact information, the company name filed on a doing business as form (if applicable), and the applicant's USDOT number. A $300 fee must accompany the application.

Surety Bond or Trust Fund

A surety bond or trust fund acts as insurance to guarantee that the shipping companies will be paid for their cargo space. If the shipper does not pay for the shipping service, the freight brokerage must absorb the cost; should they not be able to, the bond company or trust fund will cover the expense. A freight broker must have a surety bond or trust fund worth $10,000 or more.

A thorough credit and background check is generally required before a surety bond will be issued. Proof of the surety bond or trust fund is filed with the FMCSA using form BMC-84 or BMC-85.

Legal Process Agent

Freight brokerage businesses must register legal process agents for each state they operate in with the FMCSA. The process agent provides legal representation within their state, though law firms which have members in multiple states may be retained for use in each of these states. Process agents are registered with the FMCSA using form BOC-3, with spaces provided on the form for every state. A filing fee of $50 is required with form BOC-3.

IX. The Next Steps

In this training section you will learn:

Ensure Cash Flow Resources

Business Bank Account

Setting Up Your Office

IT Specs /Office Basics

Transportation Software and Other Software Considerations

Freight Broker Factoring - Helping Brokers Grow their Businesses

Freight brokers can access the capital they need to grow their business. If you have been a broker for a few months we can help you take your business to the next level. When working with us new freight brokers find it often is easier to sign up new carriers. That's because many carriers already know they will be paid for the load by the factoring company and paid the day the bills is received. Some freight brokers use this as an opportunity to negotiate discounts with their carriers. Factoring company can help you build your credit. Factoring company solid reputation helps you gain and retain more customers, it's a winning situation for us both.

Transportation Management System (TMS)

Freight broker software, also known as a transportation management system, is the computer software used to control the transportation portions of a supply chain. These software packages generally operate in three phases; planning shipments, monitoring deliveries and creating records for delivery processes. Originally, these programs monitored transportation matters only and were often stand-alone programs. Now, it is very common to find freight broker software as modules in a full enterprise management system.

The first common aspect of freight broker software is the planning of shipments and deliveries. This software helps determine when loads need to leave for deliveries or when shipments need to arrive for processing. A good piece of freight broker software will factor in variables like processing time and variation in shift production in order to ensure that the shipments arrive exactly when they should.

The second common job of freight broker software is in the execution of deliveries. This is generally the most hands-on part of the software, as it usually deals with actual people and shipments in real time. This part of the software plan routes, finds alternate methods of shipment and keeps drivers in contact with a central station. In general, this is the application of the methods from the planning phase.

The last common aspect of these software packages is as a transportation bookkeeper.

These systems keep track of the paperwork, logbooks and regulations for the company. For instance, if a particular shipment needs a driver with special training, the software will make sure one is on hand for the shipment; if a delivery requires special clearance or customs information, the software will make sure that the proper people are alerted to the issue.

While there are still several companies that make top-quality freight systems, they are much less common than they were several years ago. Many modern enterprise software packages contain a series of installable modules that cover all aspects of freight brokering. These software packages handle all aspects of a business, from development to marketing, sales, and delivery.

Generally, these programs work via separate installed modules. The basic program is essentially a shell that has only the most basic of functionality. As a company expands, it buys more modules that cover additional areas of its business. These modules all install into the original shell, keeping the company's software user-friendly and very compatible. The freight systems in these programs generally connect with other associated departments such as sales and human resources, allowing the system more freedom to recognize inefficiencies in the delivery systems.

X. Preparing Your Initial Marketing Materials

In this training section you will learn:

Determining Your Business Identity

Decide on Initial Niche Target Markets

Formulate Initial Web Site

Examples of Initial Marketing Materials

Growing a trucking or freight business comes along with its own unique sets of challenges, among which is finding effective ways to promote and market your transportation services.

Marketing is your key to a successful Freight Broker Career. Even if lack of working capital this should not hindering your freight business marketing efforts, you may be able to grow your business faster if you take advantage of these five transportation marketing ideas:

1: Know who your customers are.

Knowing "who" your customers are and what common problems or challenges they share can help you identify improvements that can make their customer experience better and – in so doing – increase their level of satisfaction and the likelihood that they will become loyal customers and refer their friends or colleagues to your transportation business.

2: Identify niche markets and ideal buyer types.

Now that you know who your customers are, you need to ask yourself if you want more customers just like them, or if you want to change up your customer mix. By thinking through demographics and characteristics that would make up an "ideal" customer for your freight business, you can better identify niche markets and target your marketing efforts to attract them.

3: Be present where new customers can find you.

Having analyzed your current customer base and identified ideal buyer types, you should also have a pretty good idea of how they did – or would be most likely to – find out about your business. Be present and make the most of opportunities to "get found" by customers and prospects:

Strategically placed and timed advertising

Listing directories - Agents or brokers

Customer referrals (do you have a reward or referral "thank you" program – do you even ask your customers for referrals?)

PPC or retargeting search engine (paid) marketing with Google AdWords, another PPC search engine or 3rd-party managed paid search marketing

Online, via internet search

4: Maximize your website's ability to attract new business.

Regardless of whether your freight business serves other businesses or the public, it's likely that the vast majority of prospects in your ideal buyer type category start searching for transportation services like yours using an online search engine (Google, Bing, Yahoo, etc.)

Check with your webmaster to be sure that your website has been equipped with the right coding and content to maximize the potential that your customers, prospects and members of your ideal buyer types will be likely to find it in an internet search online:

Keyword research to identify words and phrases that members of your target markets would likely enter into an online search when looking for a business like yours

Keyword-inspired and infused (but not stuffed!) content, Meta tags (title, description, and keywords), on-page titles and anchor link text

A blog with frequently added content (2-3x a week) that is also keyword-inspired and infused

Active presence (daily posts) on social networks where your customers are likely to have profiles, starting with Google+ and LinkedIn

Landing pages with forms (subscription forms, contact forms, request information forms, application forms) that let you capture information and begin to dialogue with members of your target markets

An active and consistently published email newsletter that (primarily) features topics of interest to your target markets and (secondarily) strategic self-promotion

5: A plan for tracking the success of your marketing initiatives and efforts.

There's an old joke in business about a company CEO who wanted to cut waste out of the marketing budget but couldn't, because, as he said, "Only 50% of my marketing is working – the problem is I don't know which half!"

Having identified your target markets and set out to reach them, it's important that you also know your starting points and measure success over time for all of the marketing tactics you use. This will help you maximize the effectiveness of what is working and minimize the waste of money, time and other resources when it comes to marketing

XI. Shipper/Carrier Process and Procedures

In this training section you will learn:

Setting Up Your Shipper Packet

Setting Up Your Carrier Packet

Setting Your Rates

Determining Competitive Rates

Resources for Rating

Rate Variables

Types of Rate Matrices

Fuel and Surcharges

Accessorial Fees

Finding Your Shippers

Load Dynamics and Operations

Building the Load

Load Data

Special Instructions

Rate Verification with Customer

Matching the Carrier

Load Posting

When to Post and What to Post

Checking Authority and Safety

Insurance Verification

Carrier Contracts

Rate Confirmation

Carrier Pick-up and Delivery

Dispatching

Tracking and Verification

There are tens of thousands of carriers operating in the United States. Your job as a broker is to identify the ones that provide the services your customers need and to confirm their reliability before using them.

ou'll find carriers listed in a number of directories and trade magazines. Word-of-
mouth is also a good way to find carriers; as you're out there networking, pay attention
to what others are saying about particular trucking companies, and follow up on good
reports.

You can also look for trucks at truck stops and on the road. When you see trucks that are
clean and well-maintained, speak to the driver and find out something about the
company. If it isn't practical to speak to the driver, make a note of the company name
and headquarters location (it will be posted on the truck or the cab), and give the
company a call.

Managing Your Accounts

From this one little question you have climbed a step on the relationship ladder. You
have struck a personal chord with your customer. From here you build on it.

As you begin to build and strengthen your relationships with your customers you will
find more and more good loads being called into you. These loads have always been
there, just handled by someone else.

The loads that you are getting when you setup a new account are the loads that your
customers find hard to move. Why would they put easy loads on the list? They know
the easy loads and more times than not pass those to their favorite transportation
provider, be it a truck or broker. This is your goal, to become your customer's favorite
transportation provider. To do this you must build a personal relationship.

As you build this relationship you'll find many shippers sharing intimate details about
their life with you. For instance, I had worked with Ed for nearly three years. His
company was about an hour away from my office, yet we had never met each other.
Over the course of time I learned of his fiancée that lived in California. He had shared
details about her visits such as how she was scared of our thunderstorms. She would
literally crawl under the bed during any thunderstorm that roared through our area.

One day he told me that she was moving to Arkansas and they had plans to marry. Once
her trip started I received play-by-play detail. She was driving this huge U-Haul truck
with her car in tow. In the truck were her two large dogs. Arizona, New Mexico, Texas,
Oklahoma and finally Arkansas, she had arrived.

Several months later I was attending a lunch meeting with a local radio station's
management and sales team. Also attending was the new Entertainment Director for
the local Civic Center. During the lunch meeting I learned that this new Entertainment
Director had just arrived from California, the San Francisco area. She had made the trip
with her two dogs in a large U-Haul truck with her car in tow.

All of a sudden this was sounding all too familiar and without thinking I popped off "...and you crawl under beds during thunderstorms." In an instant she thought that I had some special power and I though what have I done? After the initial shock cleared, we made the connection. Needless to say Ed and I met later and we became close friends. Relationships!

Keep It Going

AS you obtain accounts, loads will inevitably come. You'll have what I call gravy accounts (loads that only net about $50.00) and you'll have budget accounts (loads where you can net one, two, three hundred dollars or more). Gravy accounts are behind every corner, you have to find the budget accounts.

Not to make light of gravy accounts, they add up. But if I have a load that I can make several hundred dollars on, I'm working hard to cover that load with a truck. If someone calls about a gravy load while I'm working on the budget load, I'll sell it, but I'm not going to spend much time working it.

Now, what do I mean by working a load? Simply put, using every tool at my disposal to find a truck for the load. Working a load is much more than just posting it to the load boards and waiting for the phone to ring. It's making calls as well. This means calling trucks posted and trucks that are not posted. If I were to make a list of the steps to work a load, it would look something like this:

Post load

Rate the load

Truck search

Load boards

Approved Carrier list

Available truck list

Carrier directories

Step 1, Post load, is pretty obvious. You would post the load to your load boards. Remember, get the advertising started.

Step 2, Rate the load, is doing your math to know how much or little you're going to offer the truck to move your load.

Step 3, Truck search, has several different parts which all pertain to finding a truck for your load. Let's look at the different parts one by one.

Keep It Going

LOAD BOARDS

This is the best place to start when searching for a truck. The load boards will present trucks (equipment) that are available within a given area of your load right now. That's not to say that they're still available, just that they were at one time expected to be available in the area on a certain day. Below is an example from 123LoadBoard Match of results for a truck search within 150 miles of Atlanta, GA.

123LoadBoard

To arrive at these results we first had to create a new search. To do this we would first click the Search Trucks Tab, then the New Search Tab, located on the right. A pop-up window like the one below will appear.

Create Truck Search

Here we enter the data we wish to use in order to perform a truck search. Just as with load postings, less is more. For instance, say our load in Atlanta, GA was going to Little Rock, AR. If we were to be specific and enter Atlanta in the origin field and Little Rock in the destination field, our search would be limited to trucks meeting only that criterion. As such our results would be limited. The thinking here is that by limiting ourselves to this type of exact search, we will miss trucks wanting to go to Oklahoma City, Amarillo or other points west or in the same general area. There may be a truck wishing to go to Amarillo but can't find a load going to Amarillo. The Little Rock load may work since 1) it is going west, 2) it's right on I-40, which would be the trucks route of choice, 3) the trucking company may have another load which they can pick-up in or near the destination of our load.

So, what do we do with the destination field? I leave it blank. By leaving it blank the results will show every truck posted within the search radius chosen to all points. You pick the truck that will best suite your load and work down the list calling each. When you call a trucking company to enquire about equipment, you want to keep it short and sweet. The time to build a relationship with a trucking company is after they've agreed to take your load. Right now time is critical. You need a truck to cover your load and they need a load for their truck. As you are talking to dispatch, other brokers are calling trucking companies that are on your list seeking the same as you, a truck for their load. He, who finds a truck, makes money!

Talking to Dispatch

When you call a trucking company to enquire about their equipment postings the other KISS (keep it simple stupid) rule should apply. The conversation should go as follows:

You: This is _____ with _____. Is your truck in _____ still available?

Dispatch: Yes or No

(If no, move on to your next call, if yes, continue)

You: I have a load in Atlanta going to Little Rock, something like that work?

Dispatch: Yes or No

(If no, move on to your next call, if yes, continue)

You: (Provide details of the load providing the rate for the last detail)

Sample: It's a one pick, one drop load of lumber that needs 8' tarps. Can pick up today and deliver tomorrow. Truck needs to be able to carry 48,000 lbs. Pays $1190.00 on 530 miles.

At this point you should wait for the dispatcher to speak.

What you have just performed is a sales pitch. Just as when prospecting, you're selling. You'll find that most of your job, the making money part anyway, will be selling. As such, welcome to Sales 101. I encourage you to go to your favorite book store and buy books on selling. Even if you get one idea per book, the book has paid for itself.

Talking to Dispatch

Thirty years ago I became a salesperson. I answered a blind ad, in the newspaper, and the next thing you know, I'm selling insurance. I was put through a two week "in-house" training period. This was only to assist me in passing the test I would have to take to get my license.

During these two weeks I watched other agents come and go. They would come to the office in the morning and return in the afternoon. Every day I watched, as many of these guys were getting commission check in the morning and in the afternoon. Although I was in my early 20's, I felt like I had a lot more going on than some of these folks. This gave me the confidence to move forward, I figured that if they could do it, not only did I know I could do it, but I could do it better!

I passed my test and started selling ...well attempted to anyway. Two weeks later I hadn't sold a thing. I still had the confidence but I knew that I wasn't doing something right. I didn't have money to buy any books so I did the next best thing, went to the library. I checked out every book I could find on selling.

I read, studied, and retained the techniques that I knew I would feel comfortable using in real life. Week 3, I made money!

There's much more to this business than just knowing that you shipper needs a truck that can carry 48,000 lbs. You've got to be able to sell. A sales presentation is broken down into 3 simple parts:

The open

The presentation

The close

In the previous phone script for calling on available trucks, we find the 3 parts above in their most basic form.

The Open

You: This is _____ with _____. Is your truck in _____still available?

Dispatch: Yes or No

(If no, move on to your next call, if yes, continue)

You: I have a load in Atlanta going to Little Rock, something like that work?

Talking to Dispatch

The Presentation

You: (Provide details of the load providing the rate for the last detail)

Sample: It's a one pick, one drop load of lumber that needs 8' tarps. Can pick up today and deliver tomorrow. Truck needs to be able to carry 48,000 lbs.

The Close

You: Pays $1190.00 on 530 miles.

At this point you should wait for the dispatcher to speak.

The close is when the time has come for the customer/prospect to take action. An old rule in sales is that after a closing statement, he who speaks first loses. At this point they'll either buy or request more information. A "no" is always a request for more information unless the buyer is not qualified to make the purchase.

In this situation the dispatcher will say yes or can you pay $_____. In either case the close forces them into action.

If they were to say no it would be because the truck didn't have tarps, couldn't carry the weight or couldn't come to terms on the rate....in other words "not qualified.

APPROVED CARRIER LIST

Once you have exhausted the posted trucks on the load boards you would then turn to your Approval Carrier List. The approved carrier list is a list of carriers already set-up with your brokerage, preferably in a format searchable by state. Just as you must set-up a new customer you must also set-up a new carrier.

The first time a new carrier, new to your company, agrees to move one of your loads, you will need to exchange paperwork (set them up). To set up a carrier you will need to fax them:

Your Continuing Contract (Carrier Agreement)

Your Authority

Your Bond

A Blank W-9

Talking to Dispatch

In turn the carrier will fax you:

Your Signed Continuing Contract (Carrier Agreement)

Their Authority

Their Insurance

A completed W-9

We'll cover each of these in the Carrier Set-Up section, later.

The approved carrier list, as are the remaining truck search tools, is actually a backhaul list. A backhaul list is a tool that a broker will use to search for trucks outside of the load boards. To have a functioning backhaul list you must have:

The Trucking Company name

The type equipment they operate (vans, flats, reefer's...)

Their terminal location(s)

Their contact numbers

When using your approved carrier list, or any of the backhaul lists, if your load has a destination of Little Rock, AR, you would search and call all carriers based or with terminal locations in or around Arkansas.

What you are hoping to find is a truck that is or will shortly be available that hasn't been posted yet. When you call dispatch using a backhaul list, the conversation changes slightly:

You: This is _____with _____do you have any (type equipment needed – van, flat, refer available in Georgia today or tomorrow?

(If yes continue with the presentation, if no move to next call)

When it comes to separating the freight brokers from the order takers, those who use backhaul lists are definitely the freight brokers. The backhaul lists are not known for their high closure rate when it comes to finding a truck for your load, but they are effective.

Someday you may have a load that can net you $500.00; you will have no one to call only once. From then on, you will have some type of a backhaul list system that you have purchased or created on your own.

Truck Search and Carrier Set-up

Every day, starting with day 1 of your freight broker career, you should add carriers to the carrier database system into the Transportation Management System (TMS).

This will allow you to have trucks to call in the future should you have loads with a destination of or near the carrier's terminal. You should never throw out a carrier name.

CARRIER DATABASE

Working with Carriers

As you work your backhaul list you will want to keep your loads looking fresh on the load boards. When you're using a load board to do a truck search, you will generally call the truck that fits your load best and is the most recent posting, first. Carriers do the same thing when looking for loads. They'll call on the posted loads that best meet what they are looking for which are the most recent first.

Just as you can see how old a truck posting is on a load board, carriers can see how old your load posting is as well. As a rule, you should never allow your loads to appear to be over an hour old. Each load board has a simple way of refreshing posted loads. The load board you are using may have its own terminology for this procedure (rollover, refresh, re-post...) but it will mean the same thing. Make refreshing your loads a habit and you'll move more freight.

Contracting Carrier

As mentioned earlier, before you can use /contact a carrier, the carrier must be set-up with your brokerage. The purpose of being set-up with a carrier is to provide a type of check and balance system. Through this process you will learn if they are, in fact, a legal carrier.

Being a legal carrier is more than just having authority. It also requires that the carriers insurance be in force. For a carrier to obtain their authority they must have a minimum of $750,000.00 liability insurance and a minimum of $10,000.00 cargo insurance. This insurance must be in force at all times while operating as a commercial carrier.

Depending on your company's system, you will have a way of checking to see if the carrier is already set-up with your company or not. This could be through a phone call, using your company's web site or even a printed list. Regardless of your company's procedure, if the carrier is set-up, and everything is current, you may proceed with preparing the carrier's load confirmation.

If the carrier is not set-up with your brokerage you will need to do so in order that they may move your load. Never dispatch a truck on a load until the carrier set-up is 100% complete.

The first step to setting up a carrier is sending them what is called "your package". Your package consists of the following:

Your Continuing Contract (Carrier Agreement)

Your Authority

Your Bond

A Blank W-9

Working with Carriers

The Continuing Contract is just as the name implies a contract that continues to be in effect for all loads moved by a carrier for the broker. The load confirmations that are sent to the carrier for all future loads become a part of the Continuing Contract.

AUTHORITY

You will send the carrier your broker authority just as you did your shipper. The carrier also needs your paperwork on file to assure them that you are a legal broker.

BOND

The carrier will need a copy of your bond for two reasons. 1) For your authority to be active you must have a $10,000.00 surety bond in force. 2) Should your brokerage fail to pay the carrier they will file a claim against your bond for the amount owed them.

W-9

You will send the carrier a blank W-9 as opposed to the completed W-9 sent to your shipper. The blank W-9 is a reminder to the carrier that you will need their completed form. Most carriers will have one prepared that they will send to you with their package,

*To avoid becoming confused about what package to send to whom, it is a good idea to have two labeled folders set-up by your fax machine which contains your 2 packages, one containing the package for your shipper, the other containing the package for your carrier.

CARRIER PACKAGE TO YOU

Once the carrier has received your package, they should send you their package. Their package should include the following:

A signed copy of your contract

Their Authority

Their Insurance Accord

Their completed W-9

Working with Carriers

SIGNED COPY OF YOUR CONTRACT

This is the singed Continuing Contract you sent to the carrier with your package. It should be signed and initialed at the appropriate locations. Occasionally the carrier may try to mark out and initial a section in an attempt to change the contract. More often than not it is the section which concerns them back soliciting your customer.

Should this happen to you, call the carrier and tell them that the Continuing Contract is non-negotiable. If they continue to insist on changes, politely tell them thank you but no thanks and find another carrier to move the load. If you experience problems with a carrier early in a load, the problems will generally persist through the entire load.

As you gain experience and accrue longevity in the industry you will find that you time is a valuable commodity. There will be days when you will be on the phone, have someone holding on your cell, be answering an email and sending a package to a carrier.....all at the same time.

When this time arrives, never take shortcuts on checking the paperwork that is being sent to you by a carrier. Don't just glance at the fax machine and see the paperwork you were expecting from carrier X, and assume you have it. Pick it up and look at it. You want to check to make sure that the carrier hasn't changed anything on any of your paperwork.

Years ago I was told a story of a brokerage that had a carrier contract which had a clause which stated that the carrier would be charged a base rate of $1495.00 per year to use their brokerage. Once the $1495.00 fee was met, they, the carrier, would begin receiving payments from the brokerage for loads moved.

You can imagine the carriers' surprise when they billed the broker $800.00 for a load moved and received an invoice for a balance of $695.00 instead of a check for payment. I don't know if this ever actually happened, but it does drive home a point....Check Your Paperwork.

THEIR AUTHORITY

The carrier's authority is just as your broker authority, except theirs is a license to conduct business as a motor carrier. As such, they will have either a Common Carrier or Contract Carrier Authority. In short, a Common Carrier is required to carry insurance for the load while a Contract Carrier is contracted to his or her shipper which provides the insurance for a load.

Regardless of the type of authority, you want to do your, what I call, due diligence on the carrier. You want to check them out. With the technology available today, just about anyone with a computer can Photoshop their own authority. You want to make sure that it's real and in force. Once you receive the carrier's package you can begin the process.

Working with Carriers

The due diligence process doesn't take that long and it can save you a major headache in the long run. The first thing I will do is pull their insurance accord and call the insurance company. You'll find the companies/agent contact information on the top left of the Acord

CERTIFICATE OF LIABILITY INSURANCE

When you contact the carrier's insurance company/agent identify yourself, your company, the name of the trucking company and inform them that you need an Insurance Acord showing your company as a Certificate Holder. When you originally receive the Acord from the trucking company the Certificate Holder box will most likely be blank. Even if it is already filled in, you will still want to call the insurance company and have them send you one showing your company as a Certificate Holder. The Insurance Acord is proof that the carrier has insurance in force and for what amounts. In order for a carrier to obtain their authority they only need to have $750,000.00 liability and $10,000.00 cargo. If your shipper's load is worth $50,000.00 and the carrier only has $10,000.00, there would be a definite problem should there be a claim. Be sure that the carrier has enough insurance to cover your customer's cargo.

Should you find that the carrier's insurance is insufficient, call your contact at the carrier and let them know how much insurance the load needs and they can easily call their insurance company to have the limits increased for your load. These increased limits should reflect on the Accord sent to you from the insurance company/agent.

The Insurance Acord is a very important piece of information that you will absolutely have to have and check out PRIOR to dispatching the truck. The last thing that you want is to find out after the truck is loaded is that their insurance is not adequate.

CHECKING THE CARRIERS AUTHORITY

Now that the carriers insurance has checked out, you will want to take a look at their authority through the FMCSA website. Keep in mind that the FMCSA website is at best 2 weeks ago current. This means that the information provided about a carrier may not be 100% up to date, but it's the best we have. The FMSCA website can be found at www.safersys.org. With the carrier's authority in front of you, click the link under FMCSA Searches titled "Licensing & Insurance".

You will be asked to enter information about the carrier. Since you already have the carriers MC#, choose that search option and enter the MC# for the carrier and click search. You will be taken to their FMCSA Carrier Search results page. Here you will have the option of viewing the carrier's information via your web browser (HTML) or downloading their information in a PDF format. I always choose the HTML since it is quicker.

Working with Carriers

FMCSA

CARRIER SEARCH

Upon clicking the View Details "HTML" option, you will be taken to the Motor Carrier Details page requested for your carrier. See example below:

FMCSA

MOTOR CARRIER DETAILS

Working the Loads

When compiling your rate detail keep in mind that the rates presented are just to give the shipper an idea of what their rate would be today. Shippers know that the rate today does not necessarily mean that it will be the same tomorrow. Of course the shipper is going to try to keep rates down, but they also know that if they can't move their freight they are out of business.

Another portion of the Rate Sheet that you may or may not use is the Requested Route Rates. Your shipper may ask for a rate sheet, then add several selected loads which they move on a regular basis or perhaps they have a problem moving. In either case they wish to get an idea of what your rates would be for these loads. As you did with computing rates for origin to destination, you would do the same with the Routes (lanes). Notice at the bottom of your Rate Sheet under the "Other" section you will find:

Load/Unload: Per Load Basis - Extra Stop: $50.00 per Pick/Drop After 1st

Fuel Surcharge: Per Load Basis

Minimum Load Fee: 300 miles

Let's look at each of these individually as they will be used frequently outside of the Rates Sheet. Obviously, each is referring to added charges to the rate or the line haul. The line haul is only the amount charged to move the load from origin to destination, without any extras. As we add the extras, they are added to the line haul rate to calculate the total rate.

LOAD/UNLOAD

Loading and unloading pay is found primarily in van and refer loads. Should the driver be required to load, unload or assist in either, extra pay should be added to the rate. Normally the shipper knows this in advance and will inform you of such. The shipper generally sets a flat rate for the loading, unloading, or assisting that will ultimately add to the line haul.

EXTRA STOP

The first and last stop of a load is included with the line haul rate; however, if there are more pick-ups or drop-offs, other than the original pick-up point (origin) and the final destination, an extra charge is added to the line haul rate. This rate is negotiable between you and your shipper, but standard is $50.00 for each extra stop. For example, if you had a load that had one pick-up and two drop-offs, there would be an extra charge of $50.00 added to the line haul.

If you had a load that had two pick-ups (or picks) and two drop-offs (or drops), there would be an added charge of $100.00 added to the line haul. Remember the original pick-up and original drop-off is included in the haul.

Fuel Surcharge

An entire chapter could be dedicated to this subject; however, I'll try to keep is as simple as possible. The fuel surcharge is an added charge to the line haul, which is determined by the current average price of fuel nationwide. The Department of Energy (DOE) publishes the diesel fuel price averages every Monday on their web site at:

http://tonto.eia.doe.gov/dnav/pet/pet_pri_gnd_a_epd2d_pte_cpgal_w.htm

As a broker, the shipper will normally tell you what (if any) fuel surcharge they are paying. More times than not, you will be told that it is included in the line haul. A sample Fuel Surcharge Table can be found on the next page. In order to use the table you will need to know the average price of diesel. Let's say that it is $2.80 per gallon. Find where this price falls in the Price Per Gallon, (USD), column and find the corresponding fuel surcharge to the right in the % Surcharge column. Your fuel surcharge, at $2.80 per gallon, would be 14%. This is 14% of your line haul rate. If your line haul rate was $795.00, then your fuel surcharge would be $111.30, ($795.00 X .14 =

$111.30). The fuel surcharge would be added to the line haul with any other extras to calculate the total rate. Using our above example, using only the fuel surcharge as the only extra, your rate to the shipper would be $906.30 ($795.00 line haul + $111.30 fuel surcharge = $906.30).

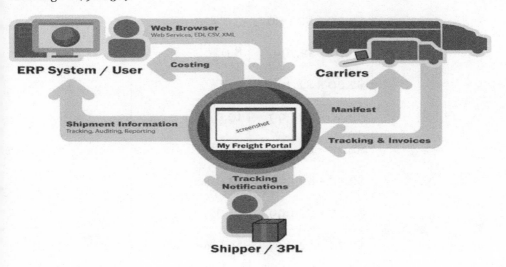

Fuel Surcharge Sample

Price Per Gallon (USD)	% Surcharge
	0.0%
$1.49 and less	1.0%
$1.50 - $1.599	2.0%
$1.60 - $1.699	3.0%
$1.70 - $1.799	4.0%
$1.80 - $1.899	5.0%
$1.90 - $1.999	6.0%
$2.00 - $2.099	7.0%
$2.10 - $2.199	8.0%
$2.20 - $2.299	9.0%
$2.30 - $2.399	10.0%
$2.40 - $2.499	11.0%
$2.50 - $2.599	12.0%
$2.60 - $2.699	13.0%
$2.70 - $2.700	14.0%
$2.80 - $2.900	15.0%
$2.90 - $2.999	16.0%
$3.00 - $3.099	17.0%
$3.10 - $3.199	18.0%
$3.20 - $3.299	19.0%
$3.30 - $3.399	20.0%
$3.40 - $3.499	21.0%
$3.50 - $3.599	22.0%

$3.60 - $3.699	23.0%
$3.70 - $3.799	24.0%
$3.80 - $3.899	25.0%
$3.90 - $3.999	26.0%
$4.00 - $4.099	27.0%
$4.10 - $4.199	28.0%
$4.20 - $4.299	29.0%
$4.30 - $4.399	30.0%
$4.40 - $4.499	31.0%
$4.50 - $4.599	

The above is a sample fuel surcharge table.

To use, if the national average fuel price is $2.50 per gallon

The fuel surcharge would be $.19 per mile.

($1.75 X .11 = $.19)

To find the national average fuel price:

http://tonto.eia.doe.gov/oog/info/wohdp/diesel.asp

Minimum Load Fee

The Minimum Load Fee (minimum line haul) is the minimum amount that you can move a load for. This is normally calculated on a mileage basis. If you notice on the load sheet, it is stated that the Minimum Load Fee: 300 Miles.

This means that a 300 mile rate is the minimum you will charge for loads less than 300 miles. Keep in mind that the shorter the load, the higher the mileage rate. Should your rate for a 300 mile load be $600.00 ($2.00 per mile), your rate for any loads shorter than 300 miles will also be $600.00. In summation, any load under 300 miles will be charged the same rate as a 300 mile load as established by the Minimum Load Fee. Any extras will be added to the line haul.

When you have completed your Rate Sheet, give it a quick review. It is recommended that you complete the Rate Sheet on your computer, print and fax to your prospect. You should also include your shipper package. Sometimes a decision by a shipper can be done in an instant, one way or the other. If your prospect has your package in hand, it could tilt the scales in your favor since all that is keeping you from obtaining a load from the shipper is, well, the shipper.

Rating a Load

Occasionally a prospect will ask "how much will it cost to move a load from point A to point B?" They are asking for a specific rate similar to the Requested Routes Rate found on the Rate Sheet.

Treat requests, from shippers of this nature, as an actual load that they have given you to move. Presumptuous? Absolutely, but on more than one occasion I have landed an account his way. The trick is not just rating the load, but working the load as if the prospect was already a customer.

Upon obtaining the information needed, in order to properly rate the load (origin, destination, weight, commodity, type eq....), you should tell the prospect that you will calculate the rate and get back with them within the hours.

The very first thing you should do is post the load on your load boards. Think of load board as advertising for your company and the products you have to offer. Your products are your loads.

There are hundreds of load boards available; however, you want the one's that will provide you the best return. Load boards range in price from free to hundreds of dollars per month. Keep in mind that for the most part you get what you pay for. We use 123LoadBoard.com, some of our agents have used others, but for our money, the three listed are the crème-de-le-crème of the load boards.

Let's say that our prospect requested a rate on a load of lumber to be loaded in Fort Smith, AR going to Conroe, TX. The weight of the load is 48,000 lbs. and the load will need to be tarped with lumber tarps. The first thing we will do is post the load with the information we have obtained. Think of it as starting our advertising.

Every load board is basically the same. Freight brokers use load boards to post loads and look for trucks posted by carriers. Carriers use load boards to post their available equipment and look for loads posted by brokers. As a freight broker, you should think of the load board as advertising your load. As with any advertising, the ad is not necessarily meant to sell the product as much as it is to get the customer in the store.

This is what you want the load board to do for you. Not sell your load but get the carrier to call you so that you can. As you can see there is a lot of information that can be posted concerning your load. You only want to post enough information so that the carrier becomes interested enough to call.

Rating a Load

As stated earlier, we want to post only enough information so that the carrier is intrigued enough to call. Just from looking at the screen, what information do you think you would want to post to achieve the desired affect? I'll list what information I post and explain why:

PICK UP DATE

Obvious due to the carrier must know the date the load is ready as it corresponds to the date his truck is empty.

TRUCK TYPE

Another obvious since the truck must be appropriate for what you customer has ordered.

ORIGIN

This is the city and state where the load is picking up.

DESTINATION

This is the final destination of where the load delivers.

FULL/PARTIAL

IS this a full load, a load that will take up most, if not all the space on the truck or a partial that will only use some of the space?

LENGTH

Full or Partial, the truck needs to know what size trailer that is needed.

WEIGHT

Full or partial, the truck needs to know how heavy the load is.

STOPS

This tells the truck how many stops there are in between loading and getting empty.

More importantly is what I didn't post.

Rating a Load

COMMODITY

I never post what the load consists of. For instance, if it is a load of lumber, a carrier might have his truck near my load but doesn't like hauling lumber. If he sees that it is lumber he won't call and I won't ever have a chance to sell him; however, if he doesn't know and calls; now, I have a chance to sell him on the idea of moving the load for me. Another reason is that I don't want the truck to find my customer on his own. This same load of lumber is loading in Poteau, OK. Instead of calling me he searches the internet for lumber companies in Poteau, OK.

RATE

Never post the rate. The reason is that if you tell how much the load is paying, automatically it's not enough and carriers won't call.

When a carrier is looking for a load they are looking for specific criteria the load must meet before they will call about it. The obvious is the origin, destination and rate. Secondly is the commodity. Lastly is how much work for the driver is involved. More often than not, if the origin and destination are right, the rest can be worked out. In our prospecting example, remember the shipper only wanted us to rate the load for them. He didn't actually give us the load; however, we took the load and posted it as if it was a real load. Now we must rate it.

Rating a Load

The 15% standard net of the $1000.00 rate charged to shipper is $150.00 ($1000.00 X .15% = $150.00). We then subtract the $150.00 from the $1000.00 to arrive at the $850.00 we are going to offer the truck.

We have our figures for the 15%, but I like to do one more with the nets figured at 10%. Using the same example, the 10% net would be $100.00, which means our offer to the truck at 10% would be $900.00

Most brokerages don't want you to go below 10% or $50.00 load nets. The reason for this is that after administrative costs, and paying the agent, the net is so low that the brokerage is actually losing money. By using the two figures (15% & 10%), you now have boundaries you can go by. In this instance you offer to the truck would start at $850.00 but not go over $900.00. Keep in mind that although 15% is standard, if you're able to get more, you should.

With the carrier rates figured, you're ready to present the load. When a truck calls you about the load you would explain the load and tell them what you are paying on the load. In our example you would tell them $850.00. You could also let them know that it was a new client and this was the first load you were working for them. If the truck agrees to the $850.00 great, in most circumstances the truck will always ask for more. Having our boundaries ready prepares us for negotiating with the truck, should the truck request more money. We know we won't pay more than $900.00, but if the truck asks for $875.00, we automatically know that it falls within what we are willing to pay.

We've actually covered a lot of ground in this one example. What we have done is actually gone through the process of working the load that is only a request for a rate by our prospect. So, why go to all the trouble?

Most brokers would have just rated the load, called the shipper/prospect back and said this is how much. What we have done is actually procured a truck for a rate that we know will work. When we call the shipper/prospect with our rate, we can not only tell them the rate, but we can add that we have a truck that can pick up the load this afternoon or in the morning.

Rating a Load

One of my first loads moved worked this way. It was a small $350.00 load that paid a $50.00 net. The shipper was so impressed that I not only picked up that load, but I landed them as a national account. They had plants across the country. That one little $350.00 load turned into a $20,000.00 a month account.

Load Types

There are three basic types of trailers with differing variations in which to haul all loads. The three would be flatbed, dry van, and refrigerated (refer).

Let's start with the Flatbed. The picture on the right is that of a loaded flatbed trailer. Flatbed loads consist of freight that is too big, heavy, bulky, or practical to load on a dry van or refer. Often flatbed loads are delivered to job sites where large forklifts or cranes are used to unload them. Loads that regularly go on a flatbed are lumber, roofing, steel, and large machinery. The variations of flatbed trailers that are derived from the basic include:

Load Types

Step deck – Loads that go on a step deck are often too tall to fit on a standard flatbed trailer. Notice how the trailer drops behind the drive axels of the truck. This allows the step deck to carry loads that would be oversize in height (13'6") on a regular flatbed.

Step deck With Risers

Carriers that have step deck equipment available may call your for regular flatbed freight. Before agreeing to load their truck, be sure that your shipper will load step decks. Often the reason a shipper won't load a step deck is that they are not able to haul as much freight or that the step on the deck presents a loading problem. To get around this problem many step decks carry "risers". These are steel frames that insert into the bed of the step deck that will allow for level loading. A picture of an extended riser can be seen above.

Load Types

Lowboy

A lowboy is designed to carry extremely heavy equipment as well as load that are too tall. Notice on the picture above the three axels on the rear of the trailer.

As you can tell there are many types of flatbed trailers, each with a specific purpose. As you start your career as a broker, you will be dealing more with the conventional type of flatbed equipment.

The most popular trailer on the road is the Dry Van. Dry vans typically haul anything that needs to stay protected from the elements. Some items that transported in a dry van are automobile parts, computers, paper products, and furniture. Dry Vans typically concentrate on full truckloads with some LTL (less than truckload) if room avails itself. More on LTL freight later. Due to the number of large trucking companies that provide dry vans you may find dry van freight to be cheaper than that of a flatbed or refer freight. Most new truck drivers start out in a dry van in order to gain experience.

Load Types

The Refrigerated Trailer, A.K.A. refer, is exactly as the name implies, a refrigerator on wheels. Meats, seafood, produce and even flowers are transported on these type trailers. Similar to a dry van in appearance, notice the large black and white box on the nose of the trailer. This is the actual refer unit.

The refer unit is powered by diesel fuel which is fed from the fuel tank located just behind the landing gear. It is advised that if you have no trucking or transportation experience to avoid refer loads for at least 6 months. Many things can go wrong with a refer load that can cost you money, should you not have the experience. For instance, many shippers and receivers require a pallet exchange. A pallet is used to place the freight on to be transported.

A pallet allows a forklift to easily move the freight between the loading dock and the truck. If you shipper told you the truck needs 24 pallets for exchange and the truck has none, there is a real possibility that you will be charged for the pallets that the truck didn't have for exchange. Pallets can cost anywhere from $2.00 to $5.00 each and up. Plus, for a pallet to be exchanged, it has to be accepted. To be accepted, it must be in good condition. So even if a truck has pallets it's not a guarantee that they are eligible for exchange. In a situation such as described above, you may not know the truck had no pallets until you receive payment from you shipper with a pallet charge subtracted from your agreed amount. Most often, by the time you find out, the carrier has already been paid. You can bill the carrier but don't hold your breath waiting for a check to arrive. In this scenario, your only hope is that the carrier provides transportation on another one of your loads so that you may deduct it from their payment. This is just one example of something that can go wrong with a refer load. This is why we advise you not to work any referring loads until you have at least 6 months experience as a broker. During those 6 months you should be learning all that you can about refrigerated freight. One more thing about refers, you will receive calls from refer carriers that may want to haul your dry load, get the ok from your shipper first. Many shippers will not load a refer trailer. Many refers, which appear to be the same size as a dry van on the outside are not the same size on the inside.

Due to insulation and the cool air shoots, the inside of a refer trailer is smaller. Check with your shipper first.

XII. Insurance Claims

In this training section you will learn:

Types of Freight Claims

Claim Forms

Claim Procedures

Claims Laws

Here is how you should file a claim with a carrier:

1. Conduct a thorough inspection of all shipments BEFORE the driver leaves and note any visible shortages, damages, or loss on the driver's delivery receipt (DR). You should not sign any delivery receipts before you have indicated such "exceptions" on the DR. If there are no exceptions simply sign and date the DR where indicated.

2. If there are exceptions, make notations on the DR as described above. Be sure and get the name of the trucking company, their address, and their Claim's Manager's name and phone number. You will need this to file the claim.

Manual method:

Caveat 1: Each step outlined ends with sending a certified letter. This establishes a paper trail in the event of a lawsuit. Consider the value of the claim before starting down this path and be sure it is worth your time and trouble to pursue.

At this point you may want to send a brief letter (via registered mail) to the trucking company letting them know you intend to file a claim. Be sure and give a description of what was lost or damaged and include copies of the DR. We also suggest you submit a Receipt Discrepancy Report along with your letter.

2. Prepare this form in four parts and distribute as follows:

Copy # 1 to the trucking company's freight claims personnel (with attached copies of respective packing list and DR's.).
Copy # 2 should be sent to your Accounts Payable Department.
Copy # 3 should be sent to your Purchasing Department.

Copy # 4 should be secured to any damaged product.

3. If there are any damage exceptions DO NOT DISPOSE of any damaged product. The carrier may wish to inspect the goods. Moreover carriers retain the right of salvage against any merchandise they may reimburse you for.

Disposing of the damaged product before the carrier releases it may void the claim. As the claimant you also have the obligation to mitigate the damages. This means if you can salvage any of the products, you must and whatever you recover is offset against the claim.

4. In all cases when damage has occurred we recommend you request the carrier to send out an inspector to examine the goods. Use the accompanying Request for Carrier Inspection Form. Submit via registered mail or some other similar method through which you can obtain a receipt. Once the carrier's inspector completes his examination, be sure and request a copy of his report.

5. When partial loss or damage is not determined until after goods are placed in inventory, you must immediately notify the carrier in writing. Typically you have 15 days to report "Concealed Damage". In addition to the standard claim form, we recommend filling out and submitting the Concealed Loss Support Document.

Submit this form immediately after the loss is discovered since you have limited time in which carriers are subject to "concealed loss or damage" claims. Send all forms via registered mail or some service where you obtain a receipt showing the carrier received your notice.

6. Ask your accounting and purchasing personnel to determine the monetary amount of loss or damage to the shipment. You will need them to provide appropriate documentation to support any invoice, repair or replacement costs.

7. Once you know the extent of the monetary loss and have received substantiating documentation from your accounting or purchasing personnel, fill out and submit to the trucking company, a Standard Form for Presentation of Loss and Damage claims. Complete this form based on the contents of the Receipt Discrepancy Report, the carrier's inspection report. Include copies of all reports and relevant documents. Be sure and submit all forms via registered mail.
8. Freight claims for loss or damage are generally governed by Title 49, CFR. Claimants must file the claim within the time limits specified in the bill of lading or contract of carriage. The time period cannot be more than 9 months (49 USC 14706e) from date of delivery or, if never delivered, the expected delivery date.

The carrier must acknowledge receipt within 30 days (49 CFR 370.5).

Carriers must pay, decline, or make a firm compromise settlement offer within 120 days after receipt of the claim (49 CFR 370.9). The time period for commencing civil action cannot be less than two years from the date the carrier gives written notice to the claimant disallowing the claim (49 USC 14706e). Since there are legal time limits for filing and processing claims, it is imperative you obtain registered mail or other receipts indicating when you filed your claim.

The government had required property and freight forwarders to maintain a minimum amount of cargo insurance and file evidence of this insurance with FMCSA. The requirement has been bodily injury and property damage liability in the minimum amount of $750,000 to $5 million depending on the nature of the cargo being transported; and cargo liability in the minimum amount of $5,000 per vehicle and $10,000 per incident.

There are another more than 150,000 motor carriers that are already exempt from the government insurance mandate for various reasons.

The federal government has required some carriers to buy cargo liability coverage since 1935. But federal law actually gives regulators the discretion whether to mandate the insurance. Jurisdiction over motor carrier and freight forwarder cargo insurance was transferred to FMCSA from the Interstate Commerce Commission (ICC) in 1999 and regulatory proposals to eliminate the requirement have been under consideration since at least 2005.

The change means that insurance companies no longer have to attach an endorsement (Form BMC-32, Endorsement for Motor Common Carrier Policies of Insurance for Cargo Liability) to cargo insurance policies.

The federal agency said it found that motor carriers typically have cargo insurance well in excess of the regulatory requirements, in part because many shippers require such insurance as a condition of doing business. Also, it said some common carriers offer shippers the opportunity to purchase additional cargo insurance and shippers have always had the opportunity to purchase cargo or inland- marine insurance directly from insurance providers rather than rely on motor carriers and freight forwarders to provide coverage for loss and damage risks.

FMCSA said it asked five insurers with the largest number of cargo policies what percentage of their clients carry more than the $10,000 aggregate minimum. All five insurers said that most of the policies they write for cargo liability are well above the FMCSA minimum. Most said their policies are for $50,000 to $100,000 liability.

Based on its inquiries, FMCSA said it believes most carriers will continue to carry cargo insurance because their customers will require it.

The only shippers that FMCSA said it considers in need of the protection provided by the cargo insurance requirement are individuals who arrange to move their own household goods. FMCSA decided that these individuals are "less knowledgeable about carrier liability requirements and need the protection afforded by the existing regulations."

The Property Casualty Insurers Association of America was among the business groups backing the change, arguing that the private insurance marketplace should determine appropriate insurance coverage.

The Owner-Operator Independent Drivers Association and the American Trucking Associations also supported the rule change.

However, shippers, shippers' freight claims collection services, transportation brokers and traffic consultants opposed the lifting of the insurance requirement, arguing that it is an important protection for the shipping public and that the BMC-32 endorsement is the only protection for shippers against high deductibles and other exclusions from liability found in cargo liability policies.

However, FMSCA sided with those who support eliminating the requirement, claiming that the move is consistent with the intent of Congress that wants "private, commercial disputes to be resolved the way all other commercial disputes are resolved– by the parties."

FMCSA also said it believes the insurance mandate may have encouraged some commercial shippers and for-hire motor carriers to conduct business inefficiently. "Shippers and motor carriers may have been taking transportation and business risks they probably would not have taken absent the BMC-32 endorsement. Carriers also may not have been spending adequately on cargo anti-theft/anti-damage systems, including training carrier personnel," the agency wrote in its final ruling.

"When this final rule becomes effective, FMCSA believes the market will improve itself. Shippers and motor carriers will begin to better assess their risks and provide better cargo theft and loss prevention measures," the agency said.

XIII Conclusion and Appendices

A Typical Day in the Life of a Broker

Broker acts as intermediaries by arranging for the transportation of cargo between shippers and carriers. Broker earns a world class income from his or her matchmaking skill.

While the business concept in freight brokering is very simple, there are many details and procedures that you need mastered. The Agent needs to know what to do, when to do it, how to do it, why it is being done and with whom to do it.

Since this is a service-oriented business, it only makes sense to learn the many demands and requirements. Especially in light of the fast-paced environment that eventually evolves. While actual "on the job" experience is the best teacher, formal training by qualified individuals helps pull everything into perspective for the beginning Broker. As a result, the Broker strikes out on a note of confidence.

Having said this, let's take a look at a typical day in the life of an Agent. After Broker has placed many prospecting phone calls and contacted as many current potential shippers as possible, he or she should have perhaps 20, 30, 40 or more shippers in their database. The initial information that each Agent will collect will be general in nature: what type of cargo is the shipper shipping, where are the normal pick up and deliver points, what kind of truck is required and so on.

1. With this information on hand, you want to setup the customer for a line of credit to ship their freight.

2. After you have educated your customers on our services, the shipper will start using you to get daily rates quotes and being shipping freight!

The next step is to follow up with the shippers to make sure our rates are ok; the shipper will go into detail on what they are looking for. Any uncertainties that the Shipper has should be cleared up immediately. It is imperative that the Agent communicates the correct information to each carrier when they start calling in.

Typical Day as a Broker

3. Then the Broker will either work up an estimate of what rate is needed and they will get back with the shipper; or the Broker will ask the shipper what they want to pay. After some calculations the Broker will come up with an amount that they will offer to the truck. The ideal starting point is to get at least a 25% profit margin on each load. But profits can run a lot more.

4. The next step is to post these loads on Load Boards to get the best rates for that day. There are numerous loading boards where loads are posted as well as searches for trucks that may be done.

5. After these loads have been posted, the agent (you) will then go to his or her database of available trucks. The Broker will then call each carrier to see if they have a truck available. In the meanwhile, the Broker may be receiving incoming calls from individuals who are responding to the posts on the loading boards.

6. At some point, the Agent is looking for the driver or dispatcher who will say, "Yes, I want the load". Sometimes the Broker will not find a truck. This is not like shooting fish in a barrel; however, with experience and by earning repeat business, the Broker will "cover" more and more loads and do so more quickly.

7. After the Broker gets the "Yes" from the carrier, he or she then immediately calls the shipper to tell them that the load is "covered".

8. The Agent (you) will then fax their set up package to the carrier. While the carrier is processing the papers, the Broker will check out the carrier to make sure the carrier is properly authorized and insured. This is done from your Broker Online Office.

9. The last item sent to the carrier is the "confirmation". The carrier should immediately sign and date this document and fax it back to the Broker.

10. Once the Broker has this confirmation on hand, the Broker will want to call the truck driver if the driver himself hasn't called the Broker. The details of the load are then given to the driver along with any other instructions. For example, the Broker will ask the driver to call when they get loaded and when they get empty or if there is any problem.

Typical Day as a Broker

The Agent will also ask the driver to call in at least every morning if it is a multi-day trip. These are important requirements that each Broker should be ready to enforce and penalize if there is a blatant disregard by the driver.

11. After the load is delivered and the carrier has reported back to the Broker, the Broker will want to call the shipper to let them know of the status.

12. Any problems on delivery, which may include missing pieces or damaged cargo, should be dealt with between the shipper and carrier. Sometimes the Broker will intervene; however, the broker is never liable for any damage or missing pieces unless the broker is negligent.

13. Lastly, with the load delivered safely and in a timely fashion, the Broker is ready to do the process over and over again.

While this routine may seem casual and boring at times - this is hardly the truth. Most of the time the Broker will experience smooth going. However, there will be times when problems will arise. Late deliveries, failure of the carrier to pick up a load, damaged cargo or missing pieces, long delays in picking up or delivering cargo - all of these need to be dealt with by the Broker.

It is impossible to avoid problems, but it is possible to stay alert and ready to deal with problems proactively. If the Broker works hard and works smart for the shipper, the Broker is well on his or her way to a successful career.

First (1st) 90 Days Strategy

Strategy for the First 90 Days

Let's Move Freight!!

Week 1: Get familiar will ALL the Lead Generation Tools. Start with 1k to 2k per month customers so that you can practice setting customers up and establishing line of credit for maximum value/time saving. The Idea here is to go through the minor fumbling of setting up a customer, credit checks, setting margins and to just get a shipment on the board.

Week 2: As you feel more confident gradually go to larger, more sophisticated shippers, perhaps 2k to 5k per month customers. Ask probing questions and qualify.

Week 3: It's a contact sport, keep it going! Follow-up with your existing shippers.

Week 4: Now that you have been trained, graduated from small to medium size customers, it is time to get the ball rolling with your customers that may require Customer Specific Pricing tariffs. Perhaps just begin with obtaining an LOA, or get credit submitted.

Week 5: Call on New Customers. Ok you have gone to your small. Medium and larger customers and are starting to get comfortable with our systems... Now go out and cold call!

Week 6: Submit your CSP Pricing and follow-up with existing shippers. It is very important to follow the CSP process in order to get pricing returned in a timely matter. Ask probing questions with your existing customers so that you can find out what questions, concerns, or road blocks they may have had with their initial shipments and experiences.

First (1st) 90 Days Strategy

Week 7-8: Call on customers. Get on the telephone and generate business. Follow-up with every customer and establish a line of credit for customers.

Week 9: Go back to your Large Customers and present to then the pricing, get them trained, and get them booking shipments. Take your time these customers, be available and attentive. Walk them through the complete functionality of 123QuoteMyLoad.com. This is important because if the entire organization is entrenched in using BrokerTranZ.com then it will be that much harder for a competitor to come in and take the business from you.

Week 10: Evaluate how you could be doing things better and follow-up with all of your existing customers. Find a way to capture more of their business.

Week 11-12: Work smart and efficiently, reduce windshield time... and Finish Strong thru your 90 day mark!

The First 90 Days

New agents need to be efficient with their time. Reduce windshield time by being strategic with how you spend your day. Route your day efficiently.

Remember there is no bad freight when you go non-asset, find a carrier for each customer!

Understand their business, get invoices, who do they currently use?

Let them know that you can enter their existing tariffs into the system!

Do not leave the office until you have asked enough questions, once you go non-asset based there are so many more options, avenues, and ways to earn/make money

Offer to be a back-up solution in case something changes with their current contacts/carriers

Remember that if you get a piece of their business that is better than none of their business

Use the phone to get into other locations and to maximize efficiency

You get credit for everything, inbound, outbound, 3rd-Party, multiple locations, etc.

It's a contact sport, go out and visit your clients, and follow-up at least monthly

Your 1st goal is to have a shipment on the board your 1st week. The 2nd weeks talk to your medium sized customers. Then start the process of getting your larger customers this should happen before your 90th day!

GLOSSARY

Accessorial

Additional charges to the line haul rate that are billed to a customer or paid to a carrier. Common accessorial include fuel surcharge, unloading charges, and stop charges

Air Bag

Large paper bags filled with air and placed between pallets or stacks of cargo to protect boxes of goods from falling to the floor or slipping within the trailer, used frequently in transporting canned drinks, especially beer.

Air Brake

A brake which is operated by air, the air is operated by the use of air lines, valves, tanks and an air compressor.

Air Freight Forwarder

Non-asset-based firm, whose primary advantage is cost, negotiate low rates with the airlines and resell in small quantities to the shippers.

Air Ride Suspension

A trailer suspension system, which uses air bags for a greater cushion than that provided by the conventional leaf spring

Backhaul

The load of freight a carrier moves in order to get back to his home terminal, or back to another direct customer, in order to get line haul rates. A broker usually arranges for a backhaul.

Bill Of Lading

Identifies: 1. The parties (consignor, carrier, and consignee), 2. The goods being transported, 3. Responsibilities of the parties, 4. The consignor or shipper typically owns the goods being transported, 5. The carrier identified on the bill of lading is the party to be paid for the freight charges and is responsible for the care of and in a safe and careful manner of the cargo, 6. The consignee or receiver is the party to whom the goods were sold to and is expecting delivery of the goods in the same condition as were shipped. 7.

The goods are typically identified, a count given and a poundage weight is given, 8. The bill of lading will normally identify responsibility for freight charges. It is the contract between the shipper and the carrier, and contains the terms and conditions.

Binders

Chain or nylon fasteners used to secure cargo to the floor of a flat-bed trailer. Usually passes over cargo and ties to the exterior sides of the trailer.

Blind Shipment

A shipment of cargo that is picked up or loaded on one bill of lading and delivered on a new bill of lading. This is done because the owner of the goods does not want the shipper to know who the receiver is or the receiver to know the shipper of the goods. Both the shipper and receiver are "Blind" to the other.

Blind Side

The right side of a truck, tractor, or trailer. This side is called the blind side because the driver's vision is restricted when he or she is behind the wheel.

Blind Spot

The area where the driver's view is blocked by part of the vehicle or other obstruction

Bobtail

When a tractor is being run without a trailer. A small single unit truck is sometimes called a bobtail. This term also refers to a straight truck.

Book the Load

An absolute commitment by broker and the customer, that broker will place a truck in a pick-up the cargo and transport it to the destination

Brokers (Transportation Brokers)

Middlemen or facilitators or intermediaries between truckload carriers and shippers. Independent contractors who act as sales agents for truckload carriers, charging a commission for each truckload they arrange.

Bulkhead

A divider placed on a load to separate portions of the product. Example: On a refrigerated trailer, you could place temperature control product in the nose of the trailer, place a bulkhead and load dry freight on the rear of the trailer.

Cab-Over Tractor

A cab-over tractor is a power unit that pulls a trailer where the driver compartment sits over the engine; the actual designation is "COE" or cab-over engine, easily distinguished from a conventional tractor, because it does not have a hood. In passenger vehicles a pickup truck would be a conventional and a van would be a cab-over.

Carrier

The trucking company hired by broker to haul freight

Carrier Information Package

Information sent via fax or the mail to a prospective carrier that gives the carrier all pertinent facts concerning broker, (our authority, bond and financial facts.)

CDL

Commercial Driver's License

Chep Pallet

Pallets that belong to the customer-receiver, usually painted blue on the ends. Loads shipped on chep pallets do not require the driver to exchange pallets at the time of loading and none will be returned at delivery point.

Class Rate

There is a class rate applicable on every product between every city pair in the country.

COFC (Container-on-flat-car)

A type of intermodal rail transportation

Consignee

In a contract of carriage, the consignee is the person to whom the shipment is to be delivered, whether by land, sea, or air.

Consignor

The consignor, in a contract of carriage, is the person sending a shipment to be delivered whether by land, sea or air.

Consolidation

Combining two or more shipments, inbound consolidation from vendors is called make-bulk consolidation; outbound consolidation to customers is called break-bulk consolidation.

Contract Rates

Agreed-upon rates between a shipper and a carrier; they trend today between large carriers and large shippers

Customer

The shipper, receiver, third-party buyer or another broker that hires a broker to handle their logistics and /or transportation needs.

Customs Broker

A highly trained import professional; licensed by the U.S. Customs Service

Deadhead

The distance a carrier travels from his unloading point to his next loading point. Example: ABC Trucking unloads their last freight in Tulsa, OK and makes his first pick-up for reloading in Fort Smith, AR. He has deadheaded 120 miles.

Detention

Stopping a shipment short of destination and diverting it to an alternate destination

Double Brokered Load

Occurs when a carrier/broker books a load directly with a broker but then sells it to another carrier/broker without booking brokers knowledge

Driver Handling

Driver being responsible for physically handling the freight, it can vary from having the driver use a pallet jack to off load or load the cargo to being responsible for completely manually loading or unloading the cargo. Our charge varies with the degree of difficulty.

Driver Qualification File

Required by DOT for every driver, includes employment application request for check of driving records from the state, request for information from previous employers, physical examination, and other documents.

Driver's Log

A record of a driver's on duty time showing his driving and on duty no driver hours

Exclusive Use

No matter the quantity of cargo being shipped, whether full trailer load, LTL, no other cargo is to be shipped with an exclusive use trailer. The customer has paid the "exclusive use" of the trailer.

Exclusive Use of Vehicle

Sometimes called modified class rates, these rates are obtained by negotiating with the carrier for an exception to the NMFC classification rating.

Expediting

Notifying a carrier that a shipment is urgent and you would like to have it rushed to destination as quickly as possible.

Flat-bed

A platform trailer that has no walls, roof, or door, the cargo is usually secured by means of chains or straps can be loaded or unloaded with or with a dock, usually used to transport machinery, building materials or extremely bulky goods that will not fit dimensionally in a van or refer trailer.

FOB (Free On Board)

Contractual terms between a buyer and a seller, which determines where title transfer takes place

FOB Destination

Title passes at destination, and seller has total responsibility until shipment is delivered

FOB Destination, Freight Collect

Title passes at destination, and buyer pays the freight

FOB Destination, Freight Collect and Allow

Title passes at destination, and buyer pay's the freight and deducts it from the seller's invoice

FOB Destination, Freight Prepaid

Title passes at destination, and seller pays the freight

FOB Origin, Freight Collect

Title passes at origin, and buyer pays the freight

FOB Origin, Freight Prepaid

Title passes at origin, and buyer has total responsibility

FOB Origin, Freight Prepaid and Charged Back

Title passes at origin; seller pays the freight and adds it on to the seller's invoice for the goods.

Food Grade Trailer

Kept in service for the transporting of food commodities, interiors are kept very clean and free of odors

For-Hire Carriers

Classified into two general categories, specialized and general freight motor carriers

Free-time on Loading/Unloading

The amount of time a carrier will wait in order to get the cargo loaded or unloaded. Normally between two and three hours before the carrier begins needing compensation, a.k.a., demurrage. Demurrage is an old railroad term that implies that charges will be accrued for using the loaded vehicles as a storage or warehouse facility for the consignee or receiver.

Freight Bill

An invoice for transportation service(s)

Freight Collect

Indicates that the consignee pays the carrier

Freight Prepaid

Indicate that the shipper pays for carrier

Gaylord

A generic and brand name of a box, approximately 40" X 40", in which loose or bulky items are shipped

Gross Vehicle Weight (GVW)

Total weight of the vehicle and its load

Hand Jack

A mechanical device used by a person to unload palletized shipments, works by pumping a hydraulic lift and manually pulling product off of trailer

Hazardous Material

A substance of material, which has been determined by the Secretary of Transportation to be capable of posing an unreasonable risk to health, safety and property when transported in commerce, they are goods that are flammable, corrosive, explosive, poisonous, bio-hazardous, radioactive or in any other way a hazard to health or safety, requires special endorsements by the Department of Transportation, the insurance company and the drive in order to be transported.

Hours of Service Regulations

All drivers must comply. Drivers must record their duty status for each 24-hour period. They may not legally drive more than 11 hours following 10 consecutive hours off duty.

Inbound Consolidation (make-bulk)

Occurs by having your vendors in a particular area deliver LTL to a local assembly center, then the consolidated truckload is shipped to destination. This is much cheaper than having the vendors ship each individual small shipment LTL.

Independent Operator

A truck owner that operates under his own authority and usually finds own freight

Intermodal

More than one mode of transportation is involved (e.g., piggyback, fishyback, or birdyback).

International Freight Forwarders

Also called foreign forwarders or ocean freight forwarders; handle booking, paperwork, and consolidations for   exporters.

Interstate

Crossing state lines in order to make deliveries, example: ABC Trucking loads furniture in Conway, AK to be delivered in Columbus, OH

Intrastate

Making all pickups or deliveries within one state, example: trucking loads of furniture in Conway, AK to be delivered in Hot Springs, AK

Jackknife

When the tractor is not in a straight line with the trailer, that is, the trailer is not right behind the tractor.

Jack Brake

An engine brake used to slow the vehicle

JIT (just-in-time)

Focuses on the systematic reduction of waste and inefficiencies in operations to improve overall performance, the end result is the delivery of products at just the right place, in just the right quantity, and at just the right time.

Landing Gear

A device that supports the front end of a semi-trailer when it is not hooked to a tractor

Layover

The amount of time spent between last unloading and reloading, layover time is usually used to catch-up on service hours and paperwork (overnight).

Lease Operator

Someone who owns his or her own tractor but signs a contract or lease to haul for one company

Less Than Truckload (LTL) Carriers

Maintain a network of freight terminals and a large staff of dock workers to handle small shipment as they are loaded and unloaded

Line Haul

The load of freight a carrier normally carries out of his home terminal for a customer

Load Locks

A securing device to hold cargo in place in a van or refer trailer, it is usually made of aluminum poles and extends from one wall to the other and has a ratcheting device that holds it in place.

Loading

The act of filling a trailer with the shipper's goods normally accomplished by mechanical means (forklift) but can be done manually

Log Book

As required by law and for the safety of the public (you) a truck driver is only allowed to work or drive a certain amount of time every day or in a series of days. A log book is the record of his time and made available to public safety personnel in order to verify that he is not in violation of any safety laws

Logistics

The process of planning, implementing, and controlling the efficient, effective flow and storage of goods, services, and related information from point of origin to pint of consumption for the purpose of conforming to customer requirements.

Lumper

The party who actually unloads the goods off the trailer, a receipt for this labor is required before any reimbursement will be made. Most consignees' will off load their goods and not charge for unloading the cargo.

Mileage Rate

Rate per mile offered by truckload carriers

Military Time

A 24-hour time frame where its appropriate number designates each hour, 0100 to 2400

Minimum Charge

The lowest charge that can be assessed for a particular movement, regardless of the weight

NAFTA

The North American Free Trade Agreement was signed by leaders of the United States, Canada, and Mexico in December 1992; it that will phase out tariffs (import duties) among the three countries over the next 15 years.

National Motor Freight Classification (NMFC)

-Class rates are based on the NMFC, and virtually all shipments are subject to class rates. Every product that can be shipped is assigned a class rating; also contains rules pertaining to claim filing procedures, packing provisions, handling and service

Non-Asset-Based Third-Party Providers

Do not own assets, such as transportation and/or warehouse equipment

Nose of a Trailer

This is the front or portion located closest to the tractor.

NVOCC – Non-Vessel Operating Common Carrier

Consolidates small shipments from different shippers into full container loads and arranges all details from origin to foreign delivery

O.S.D. (Overage, Shortage or Damage)

The first question you ask when the driver on your load or freight calls in to report empty. He'll understand, "Any O.S.D.'s?" What you are asking has to do with the condition of the freight when it was received at the consignee(s). If the driver's reply to your question of "Any O.S.D.'s?" is "NO, all clear", this means that the bill of lading or proof of delivery has been received and that no problems exist.

Off-Duty Time

The time a driver is required to be ready to work or, when working, the time until a driver is relieved from work and all duties.

On-Duty Time

The time a driver is required to be ready to work or, when working the time until a driver is relieved from work and all duties

Out of Service

Authorized personnel shall declare and mark "out of service" any motor vehicle, which by reason of its mechanical condition or loading would likely cause an accident or a breakdown. An "Out of Service Vehicle" sticker shall be used to ark vehicles "out of service"

Outbound Consolidation (breakbulk)

Consolidation of a number of small shipments for various customers into a full truckload, shipped to a location near the customers; then has the carrier distribute the small shipments to the customers.

Pallet Block

Term used to describe how many cases are stacked per layer on a pallet

Pallet Exchange

A requirement by some customers, that the cargo will be pre-loaded on wooden pallets for shipment and the carrier is required to turn in empty pallets to turn in empty pallets for the next shipment. In the event the carrier does not have empty pallets to turn in for deposit on a pallet exchange load a charge of from $4.00 to $10.00 each is usually taken from the carrier. Upon delivery of a pallet exchange load the carrier, in like manner, should receive empty pallets from the consignee.

Pallets

A platform on which cargo is stacked in order to facilitate loading and unloading, openings in which a forklift can lift, are made on all four sides of the pallet, standard size 48" X 40", but many other dimensions are manufactured.

Parcel Shipments

The smallest truck (and air) shipments, which are by far the most expensive in terms of cost per unit (per pound or hundredweight)

Pickups and Stop-offs Destination

Any extra loading points past the point of origin are extra pickups. There is a varying charge for this service. In like manner, any drops of cargo before final destinations are considered stop-offs. Likewise, there are varying charges for stop-offs. The customer is never charged for the loading at origin or delivery to the final drop (stop).

Pig Tail

The cable that carries electrical power to the trailer from the tractor

Port of Entry

Points in a state, normally on a major highway, where commercial vehicles enter and are checked by public safely personnel to make sure that all licenses, permits, log books, weight restrictions, vehicle inspections or any other matter concerning safety or interstate commerce are adhered to before entering that state. (When transporting perishable goods or live animals that all paperwork and inspections have been made.)

Prepay and Add

The seller pays the carrier and adds the freight charges onto the invoice for goods purchased.

Private Carriers

Those motor carriers whose primary business is other than transportation manufacturers or distributors who use their own private business

Proof of Delivery (P.O.D.)

A receipt by the consignee for the goods and condition of it

Public Warehouse

A firm that specializes in warehousing and hold itself out to serve the public like a for-hire carrier. One pays only for space used.

Receiver

Also know on the bill of lading as the consignee, the party taking possession of the goods when they are unloaded off of the trailer.

Reciprocity

Authority to enter border provinces of Canada

Re-consignment

Changing the consignee in transit, carrier charges the shipper for this service.

Refer

A van trailer with the addition of a refrigeration or cooling unit and insulations in the walls, sides, roof, floor, and doors, can be used to transport perishable goods (produce, meats, dairy goods, etc.) or dry or non-perishable goods. Because of the insulation in the walls, roof, and floor the refer trailers lose s some load space.

Reverse Logistics

A specialized segment of contract logistics management; the back side of logistics, logistics after the sale and after the initial delivery to the customer

Roll Up Door

Door made into sections that roll on a track, when opened this door is suspended from track inside of the trailer. This type of door reduces clearance level for cargo.

Roll Up Doors

A roll-up-door is like a garage door that rises vertically to allow for the loading of cargo. A roll-up-door is normally seen on city pickup and delivery trailers.

Routing Guide

Instructions for the supplier concerning carrier to use and other requirements

Scale Tickets

A Certification of weight of the tractor/trailer handle and handle base to prevent undetected entry to a trailer.

Semi-Trailer

A trailer with wheels in the back, the front of the trailer rests on the rear of a tractor.

Shipper

Also known on the bill of lading as the consignor, usually the manufacturer of the goods being shipped on the trailer

Skid

Another term used by driver's for pallets.

Sleeper

That portion of a tractor used as rest or sleeping quarters.

Slip Sheet

A very thick, normally one inch, piece of cardboard on which cargo is stacked. Used much like a pallet, requires a slip sheet machine to lift the cargo and place on or off the trailer.

Specialized For-Hire Truck Carrier

Transports heavy machinery, liquid petroleum, refrigerated products, agricultural commodities, motor vehicles, building materials, household goods, and other specialized items

Spread Axel

Refers to an axel on a trailer that is spread more than 108 inches apart

Stop-Off Consolidation

The consolidation of several large shipments in which the carrier may pick up or deliver while in transition to a large consignee. A premium is charged for this service.

Straight Bill Of Lading

One, which is non-negotiable; the contract between shipper and carrier for a shipment direct to a consignee

Tail Gate Delivery

When a driver is required to deliver product from within the trailer to the rear of the trailer so the receiver can accept it from his own dock

Tail of a Trailer

The back end area or rear of the trailer

Tarp

A nylon or plastic or canvas blanket used to cover shipments on flatbed trailers to protect from pilferage and weather damages.

Team

When there are two drivers working together on a truck

Terminal

The city that a carrier based in or the city in which the truck is based

Third-Party Logistics (3PL)

A 3PL is easily defined as a Travel Agent for freight. A broker act as consultants for customers on how to move their freight from point A to point B with ease and advises the most cost efficient transportation mode available to them. Brokers negotiate with the customer on a price and then pay carriers a lesser rate.

Time-Critical Shipments

Non-stop, door-to-door delivery; not co-mingled with freight of other shippers

Time-Definite Services

Delivery is guaranteed at a certain time of the day, shippers pay a premium, for this service

Tracing

Trying to locate a shipment that has been reported undelivered by the consignee; finding the current status of the shipment. Tracing has become more effective through the use of EDI (electronic data interchange).

Tractor

The power unit needed to pull the trailer.

Truck Ordered Not Used

Compensation for sending a carrier in for loading and the cargo is not ready for shipment within a reasonable time and the truck order is canceled.

Truckload

Carriers handle approximately 41 percent of all truck shipments (volume) and earn 37 percent of total truck revenues.

Unit

The refrigerated unit mounted on trailers for temperature control products

Unloading

The reverse of loading, taking the goods off of the trailer and putting it in the receivers' warehouse, normally done mechanically but can be done manually.

Van

An enclosed or box van is our primary means of transportation. Length varies from 45-57 feet. It has a wooden floor with sides and a roof. Exterior width varies from a 96 to a maximum of 102 inches. The load space on a regular 48 X 102 trailer is 47.5' X 8.0' X 9.2' or 3480 cubic feet. Used to transport non-perishable goods, (paper goods, manufacturing goods, furniture, etc.).

Vented Trailer

A trailer with holes in the front and in the rear doors to facilitate the flow of air across the cargo and keep ventilate, used normally in transporting semi-perishable goods (potatoes and watermelons).

Wash Out

When trailer is power washed on the inside to remove dirt and debris from the walls and floor.

Air Freight - Declared Value and Insurance

Question: We send shipments out by air freight and will declare a value of $1,000.00 per shipment, which is the amount of our insurance deductible, even though the value may be much greater. The question is, have we prejudiced our ability to collect the invoice value from the insurance company by only declaring a $1,000.00 value on the air way bill?

Answer: By declaring a lesser value on the air waybill, you have prejudiced your insurer's ability to recover the full invoice value from the carrier through subrogation. You would have to review the particular insurance policy as some policies allow the shipper to ship under a bill of lading with a released rate or limitation of liability, and some do not.

Is the shipment domestic or international? The liability differs. Domestic could be 50 cents per lb., 50 cents per lb. per piece, or $9.07 per lb. per piece. International is now 17 SDR's per kilo, or about $10.41 per lb. per piece.

As to the declaration on the air waybill, if you declare the value at $1,000, the carrier will assess an excess value charge for the amount of value that exceeds its tariff limit, whatever that may be. For example, if a shipment weighs 500 lbs. and has an invoice value of $5,000, that's $10 per lb. But if the airline's liability is only 50 cents per lb., or $250, it will charge its excess value charge for $750.00. That could be 35 cents to $1.00 per $100 of excess value, depending on the carrier's tariff. ($26.25 to $75.00)

It may be cheaper to have the insurance deductible set at the carrier's liability limit. The shipper would file claims against the carrier for its tariff limit, and the insurer will pick up the losses over that limit. Insurers' premiums are usually much cheaper than carriers' excess value charges.

As to your question about the insurer's subrogation claim against the airlines, the insurer must claim the actual invoice value of the loss. However, the airline will only pay up to the limit of its liability unless a higher value has been declared. If you are successful in changing your insurance policy as suggested above, there will be no need to file claims against the airline, as you will recover up to the limit of the airline's liability.

Air Freight Forwarder - Liability for Theft

Question: An airfreight forwarder has declined our claim on the ground that it has no liability for thefts! Is this correct?

Answer: Definitely not. Air freight forwarders that issue their own house air waybill are liable as common carriers. Even if there were some exculpatory clause in the forwarder's unfiled tariffs, it would be unenforceable.

Bar Code Errors

Question: When a shrink-wrapped pallet does not clear a bar code scanner, should it be noted as an exception on the delivery receipt?

Answer: Yes, as a precautionary measure. It would not be proper to report that pallet as a non-delivery - merely report the fact that it would not scan properly. If there is evidence of damage, shortage or breaking of the packages or shrink wrap, it should be surveyed and noted.

Bills of Lading - "Straight" vs. "Order"

Question: What is the difference between a "straight" bill of lading and an "order" bill of lading?

Answer: A straight bill of lading requires the carrier to deliver the freight to the named consignee. It is a "non-negotiable" bill of lading.

An order bill of lading is a negotiable document which represents title to the goods. It can be endorsed by the "order" party to transfer title to the goods to a third party. It must be physically surrendered to the carrier before delivery.

Brokers - Withholding Payment for Claim on Prior Load

Question: We are a motor carrier and carried a load a couple of months ago contracted through a broker.

After delivery, I billed the broker for the amount agreed upon in the rate confirmation and submitted a signed, clear BOL. They, in turn, sent me payment for the load.

I was informed a week ago, there was a claim on the load for damages. Now, they are withholding payment on another load. My questions are: Can the broker withhold payment on the other load? Can the shipper file a claim for damages when there is a clear BOL?

Answer: As to your first question, the broker cannot withhold payment of freight charges which are due. The broker has no ownership interest in the shipment, and is merely a middleman who arranges for transportation.

Regarding the claim for loss or damage, the fact that there was a clear delivery receipt does not preclude the shipper or consignee from filing a claim. It could be "concealed damage" which was discovered after delivery. The clear delivery receipt does place a greater burden on the claimant, to prove that the loss or damage could not have occurred after delivery. Note also that the bill of lading requires that the claimant file a claim in writing with the carrier, with appropriate supporting documentation.

Brokers - Assumption of Liability for Loss & Damage

Question:

1.   Is it OK if our broker says it will pay all claims (rather than the carrier) and is willing to sign an agreement to that effect? Can a broker assume liability for claims under a contract and what if the broker's insurance company refuses to pay?

2.   Our agreement states that the broker is compensated by the carrier on freight bills paid by shipper to broker. The broker dislikes this language, but this was written to reduce the exposure resulting from having the broker act as an agent for the shipper. Can we do this?

A:

1.   a. I see no reason why a broker cannot assume liability for loss & damage claims as part of its contract with the shipper.

b.   Contractually assumed liability would probably not be covered by most "contingent cargo liability" policies. It would be necessary to review the broker's insurance policy to be able to give a definitive opinion.

c.

2. It is common for the shipper to pay the broker, and the broker to pay the carrier, retaining its "commission" (profit) out of the spread. When carriers are not paid by the broker, they often try to collect from the shipper, arguing that the broker acted as the agent of the shipper.

Thus, shipper-broker contracts and broker-carrier contracts sometimes include language to the effect that the broker acts as the agent of the carrier for purposes of collecting freight charges.

Brokers - Caught in the Middle

Q:

We are an exempt freight broker and have been getting stuck in the middle between our customers demanding that we pay freight claims and the carriers demanding that we pay the freight charges, even though there are damage claims on the shipment. What should we do?

A:

As a freight broker, you are legally considered an "independent contractor". You are not a shipper and you are not a carrier. You should always make this clear to the people you deal with.

In order to avoid these problems you should enter into written agreements with both your shipper customers and the motor carriers that you use. Such a contract would make it clear that you are not liable for loss or damage, and that the shipper has primary liability for the freight charges (as well as other relevant provisions, which are agreed to in the contract).

Brokers - Liability for Non-Delivery

Q:

I brokered freight from Los Angeles to Pennsylvania.   Prior to giving the load to the carrier we obtained their authority and insurance, and then sent them a confirmation for pickup and delivery which they signed and faxed back. After missing their 3rd scheduled appointment for delivery, they informed us by letter that the freight rate had ncreased and that they must have payment prior to delivery. We offered to have a ashier's check at the consignee's dock when they delivered, which they refused and ubsequently their phone has been disconnected and they have disappeared with the reight. We have contacted authorities for help without success.

The carrier's insurer is denying the claim on the basis that their client will not respond, and I'm not sure my contingent cargo insurance will cover us. What can we do?

A:

nitially, as a broker, you should not be in the middle. The shipper or owner of the goods s the proper one to bring a claim against the carrier. As a broker, you have no property nterest in the goods and are not a party to the contract of carriage (bill of lading). This loes not, of course, prevent you from assisting your customer with the claim.

Second, from the facts as stated, the shipper has a legal action against the carrier for the non-delivery of the shipment, and also probably for "conversion", but it would be necessary to get a lawyer, and commence a lawsuit. Even though the carrier appears to have disappeared, the carrier's insurer would probably step in to defend and/or pay the claim.

Third, depending on the value of the shipment, it might be worth filing a claim against the carrier's BMC-32 cargo endorsement.

Finally, with regard to your broker's contingent cargo policy, it is our experience that many of these policies have so many exclusions and conditions so as to be almost worthless. However, you should never take "No" for an answer; if necessary, you can also sue your insurer to enforce the policy provisions.

Brokers - Licenses

Q:

We are considering getting a brokerage authority. Where do we get the form and what else do we need? We are a grain elevator using mostly hopper trailers. We would appreciate any help you could give us.

A:

The Interstate Commerce Act requires that brokers for the transportation of property must "register" with the Department of Transportation

The FMCSA has established regulations governing applications for broker registration.

Brokers - Name on Bills of Lading

Q:

When we ship with a broker, should their name be on the bill of lading or the carrier's?

Also, if we put the language from the TCPC's Shipper's Domestic Truck Bill of Lading, "Carrier designates broker"... on our bill of lading, is this a legal agreement between the shipper and the carrier if both the shipper and the carrier (driver) sign the bill of lading?

A:

1. There is no problem with putting the broker's name on the bill of lading; so long as you don't show it as the CARRIER. If you do put the broker's name on the bill of lading, qualify it with the word "broker" to indicate the proper capacity.

2. While there are many variations of the bill of lading today, technically only carriers that are "participants" in the NMFC are required (or permitted) to use the Uniform Straight Bill of Lading in the Classification. Even if the carrier is a participant in the NMFC, Item 362 permits the parties to use alternative forms such as TCPC's Shipper's Domestic Truck Bill of Lading. Utilizing the language "Carrier designates broker..." can help avoid problems, but absent a prior agreement with the carrier, there is no guarantee that the carrier will honor such language based upon the signature of a driver. TCPC's "Shipper's Domestic Truck Bill of Lading" comes in a kit which explains the use of the bill of lading and recommends that the shipper get the carrier's prior agreement to use that form of the bill of lading.

Brokers - Protecting Shippers' Interests

Q:

We occasionally have the need to utilize the services of a transportation broker to secure flatbed trucks. I would like to know the proper way to utilize the transportation broker and to make sure that our company is protected against false claims. In the past, we have received a quotation, given the final destination to the broker, requested and have received certificate of operating authority, and copy of the carrier's insurance. We also put the name of the broker on the bill of lading as the transportation company and we pay the bill timely.

We had a problem recently when we received a telephone call from the carrier requesting payment, as they claim they had not received payment from the broker. We told them to call the broker as we paid our bill. How we can protect ourselves?

A:

This is a problem that continues to arise and first, you should always know the party with whom you are dealing.

Always get a copy of the broker's license and if there is any doubt, check with the FHWA to make sure that the information is current and the broker has a surety bond on file. You can call for registration and insurance information. You may also check with the Transportation Intermediaries Association to see if the broker is a member and is in good standing.

Second, we recommend that shippers who use brokers insist on a written shipper-broker contract, and that the brokers have written contracts with their carriers. This is the best protection.

An alternative is to use TCPC's "Shipper's Domestic Truck Bill of Lading" which contains the following language in the terms and conditions: "If transportation is arranged through a broker, Carrier designates broker as its agent for the collection of freight charges. When charges are paid to broker, Carrier agrees not to hold shipper or consignee liable for said charges."

Third, I would not recommend that you show the broker's name as the carrier on the bill of lading. If you show the broker's name, indicate "broker" to show the correct legal capacity.

Fourth, unfortunately, the "double payment" problem is very common when brokers go out of business or abscond with funds. This is a "gray area", but the general rule is that if the shipper has dealt only with the broker, and has paid the broker, the carrier cannot come back to the shipper to collect its freight charges.

Brokers, Agents and Third Party Logistic Providers

Q:

What are the differences between intermediaries such as Brokers, Agents and Third Party Logistic Providers? Also, how can we protect from liability, claims and billing chargebacks (when an intermediary does not pay and the carrier comes after you).

A:

Your question cannot be easily answered in a brief message.

With regard to liability for freight charges, the law is quite different depending on whether you are dealing with a freight forwarder, broker, etc. As a general rule, if you are dealing with a freight forwarder and you pay the forwarder, you should have no liability to the underlying carrier(s) for freight charges. If you are dealing with a broker, and you pay the broker, but the broker doesn't pay the carrier, you could possibly be liable to the carrier depending on the factual issues.

In the case of a shipper's agent or a shipper association, the shipper generally will remain liable to the carrier if the agent or association does not pay the carrier.

Bumping Privilege - NMFC Item 171

Q:

What is a "bumping privilege" under the NMFC's rules, and what does it mean?

A:

Item 171 of NMFC 100-Y, the latest issue effective Oct. 17, 1998, allows a shipper to increase the weight of its shipments to artificially increase package density so that it may apply the next lower class in a density scale and thus obtain a lower rate. The applicable tariff must make reference to this Item, and this may be done only at the time of shipment.

Bumping Privilege - Limited to Shippers

Q:

Can a consignee take advantage of the "bumping privilege" in NMFC Item 171 upon delivery?

A:

No. The language of item 171 is quite specific and is limited to action taken by the shipper at the time of shipment. The obvious answer for consignees on collect shipments is to notify their shippers to be aware of the rule and take advantage of the bumping provision at the time of shipment.

Carmack Amendment - Who is Covered?

Q:

Which carriers are currently subject to the Carmack Amendment? Are UPS and Federal Express subject to it?

A:

Yes, all carriers subject to the DOT's regulation are subject to Carmack, including the surface operations of UPS and Federal Express. Some of their claim policies are in violation of government regulations, and could be changed if enough support were generated among shipper groups.

Carrier Holding Freight "Hostage"

Q:

I made three shipments via a broker, who, in turn, gave the shipments to a motor carrier for delivery. After two weeks, the freight had still not been delivered. When the freight finally did arrive at the intended location, the pallets were triple stacked, and had fallen over. There were parts scattered all over.

The carrier told me they would restack the load and redeliver, but they never did. I called the broker and told them to get my freight back. The carrier told the broker that they would do it . . . FOR $7,800.00.

I have a big problem. None of my shipments were delivered and I am being blackmailed for their return.

Is it the responsibility of the broker to get my freight back or am I screwed?

Any help would be most appreciated as this has been going on for a number of weeks and now the carrier has faxed me a letter saying it was going to cost me $100.00/day for storage until I pay for the freight.

A:

Unfortunately, your story is not unusual.

First, you have to recognize that a motor carrier has a "lien" for freight charges on any shipments it transports and does not have to release the shipment until its charges are paid. In your case, the carrier can probably hold your cargo hostage until the charges are paid. You probably have to tender payment of their charges before they release the shipment. Then, your recourse for the loss or damage to your freight is to file a written freight claim with them and, if necessary, bring a lawsuit to collect your damages.

You may also want to question the amount of the freight and/or storage charges and see if they are charging you based on their correct tariff rates; it is quite possible you may have been overcharged.

As to the broker, your recourse is limited. A broker is not a carrier; it is only an intermediary and, as such, is not generally liable for loss or damage to your cargo. The only exception is when the broker is clearly negligent - such as selecting an unsuitable carrier with a bad safety rating or no insurance. I am surprised, however, that your broker did not try to intercede for you and try to work something out with the carrier. My guess is that the broker and carrier are not on good terms.

Carrier Use of Shipper's Forklift

Q:

What kind of liability is the shipper subject to when the carrier's driver uses the shipper's forklifts to load shipments into or onto the carrier's trailer? If there is an injury is it a workman's compensation issue or something else?

A:

This is not a "transportation law" question. This falls into the general area of liability for negligence to a business invitee, i.e., anyone on your premises for normal business purposes.

Most shippers don't allow anyone other than their own employees to operate their equipment.

In theory, the shipper could be liable in negligence to a truck driver if it provided an unsuitable or defective piece of equipment such as a fork lift for his use, resulting in injury to the driver. While the driver's claims against his employer (the trucking company) would be subject to Workmen's Compensation, the driver could have a cause of action for negligence against a third party, i.e., the shipper.

CDL Licensing

Q:

I'm requesting information on CDL positions and requirements. Thank you for your assistance in this matter

A:

CDL licensing procedures vary from state to state. I would suggest that you contact the local department of motor vehicles where you live and get the application forms and information from them.

Claims - Mitigation of Damages

Q:

A door assembly for an off-road haul truck was damaged when we received it and it was noted on the freight bill. Because the customer could not wait for the claim to be resolved, we had to order another door for the customer. Now the freight carrier wants us to have the door repaired, which we don't want to do for several reasons:

First, our customers would not want a repaired door; second, off-road haul trucks fall under rules and regulations regarding the modification of roll over structures, and this door is part of the roll over cab and should not be modified; finally, we only sell one of hese doors maybe every ten years or so and have no outlet for it. The freight carrier has been inflexible in this matter. What can we do to get our $1600.00 dollars back?

A:

This is a tough one. The problem is that a consignee receiving a damaged item usually has a duty to "mitigate the damage" if it can reasonably be done. Normally this would involve repairing or refurbishing a damaged item, or sorting and segregating damaged/undamaged items.

The legal test is whether your actions were "reasonable under the circumstances". I would say that you do have some good reasons for purchasing another door for your customer. The only thing that I might suggest is to contact the door manufacturer and see if they will take it back for some kind of salvage allowance. They would probably be in a better position to repair and resell the door.

As a last resort, of course, you may have to bring a lawsuit against the carrier. From the size of the claim, you may be able to do this in a local small claims court.

Claims - Prepaid Freight Charges

Q:

We include prepaid freight charges with our loss and damaged claims. We did not charge the customer for the freight. Two carriers have denied the freight portion of our claims on the premise that the merchandise value includes the cost of the freight. Our merchandise moved Prepaid-FOB nearest warehouse. The freight is paid by us and it is not in the price of the product. In light of this, is the carrier obligated to pay the prepaid freight charges?

A:

I think the carriers may be correct on this one. You have apparently priced your product so that the selling price to the customer is sufficient to cover the anticipated cost of freight which you are separately paying to the carrier.

Look at it this way - if the customer had risk of loss in transit (FOB origin), and the goods were lost by the carrier, the customer would have to pay you the invoice price only, and would not also have to pay the freight charges.

The customer's claim against the carrier would be for the invoice price. Why should the amount of damages be different depending who files the claim?

Claims - Recovering Freight Charges on Partial Deliveries

Q:

On partial deliveries, can I recover the freight charges on the missing cartons as a part of my claim?

A:

Yes. Claimants are to be made whole when shipments are delivered short or damaged. You are entitled to add a prorata share of the total freight charges based on the weight of the missing cartons. If the shortage is to be replaced with another shipment which costs more freight due to the smaller size shipment (LTL, for instance, rather than the original TL shipment), you are entitled to recover the extra freight cost from the carrier as your measure of damage.

Claims - Regulations and Procedures

Q:

We are not having much luck recovering loss and damage claims. It seems the carriers either decline the claims or simply fail to respond. What do you suggest?

A:

Motor carriers are subject to federal regulations governing claims: "Principles and Practices for the Investigation and Voluntary Disposition of Loss and Damage Claims and Processing Salvage.

The regulations outline the procedures that are supposed to be followed and include specific time limits in which action is to be taken.

Unfortunately, since the demise of the I.C.C., there is little effort to enforce these regulations and they are often ignored.

We suggest that you enter into properly drafted contracts with your carriers that include provisions for the handling of L&D claims.

Claims - Repackaging Expenses

Q:

A carrier delivered part of a shipment late. The consignee refused the freight because it was late.

Since the cartons were labeled for that specific consignee the cartons required repackaging. The carrier refuses to pay for repackaging, but they would "consider a reasonable restocking fee." Since the freight was delivered late and refused shouldn't the carrier be liable for the repackaging expenses?

A:

 This claim falls into the category of a "delay claim", and the legal issue is whether the damages (your repackaging expenses) are "foreseeable" at the time of shipment. If they were, they are recoverable.

I would think that the need to repackage, relabel, etc. if shipments are rejected due to carrier delay would be a reasonably foreseeable consequence of the delay. Certainly, it can be argued that you have mitigated your damages by putting the goods in a condition that they can be resold to another customer.

The carrier should pay these repackaging expenses.

Classification of Shipments

Q:

How do we determine the correct "Tariff Code" when shipping plastics and rubber products to Canada and Mexico?

A:

It is not clear what you mean by "tariff code".

If you are talking about the proper identification of an article on a motor carrier bill of lading, the usual way is to refer to the National Motor Freight Classification which lists thousands of "articles" and sets forth the "class" which is used for rating the shipment. If you do not have a copy of the Classification, or are unfamiliar with it, seek answers from a transportation consultant.

If you are talking about how to describe articles on an export document, contact a freight forwarder dealing in exports to Canada or Mexico.

Common Control - Shipper and Broker

Q:

May a shipper own or have an interest in a broker?

A:

No, the former ICC's regulations (now FHWA) prohibit brokers from receiving compensation when they own a shipper, where the shipper owns the broker, or when there is a common ownership of the two.

Concealed Damage - Canned Goods

Q:

I have a question concerning concealed damage on canned goods.

We have a shipment that we consolidated with both refrigerated and dry product. We specified and paid extra for a bulkhead to protect the dry product from freezing. The shipment was delivered to our customer in south Florida (hot and humid). It was delivered with no exception on the bill of lading.

Several weeks later our customer informed us that the cans were rusting and seeks to file a claim against the carrier.

My question is this: Can we file a claim for concealed damage or would this be considered inherent vice of this product.

A:

From your description of the facts there is no evidence that the cans got wet while in the truck, or that they were wet at the time of delivery. It would seem that, most probably, moisture condensed from the atmosphere onto the cold cans after they were delivered and that they remained wet for a long enough period to cause rust.

I don't see how the carrier is responsible for this. After all, it was the shipper who decided to ship both refrigerated and dry product in the same truck. Also, the consignee might have prevented the rusting by opening the cartons and drying off the cans, or by storing them in a dryer atmosphere.

Concealed Damage - Clear Delivery Receipt

Q:

Can a carrier refuse to participate in concealed damage claims? I filed a concealed damage claim and the carrier was notified a few hours after delivery of the damaged goods. The carrier replied that they will not participate in any claim where they have a clear delivery receipt. Is this legal?

A:

The fact that damage may be "concealed" does not relieve the carrier of its duty to conduct a proper investigation of the claim. This requirement is set forth in federal regulations which are binding on all interstate motor carriers.

Contracts - Consignee-filed Claims

Q:

We have a contract provision that reads "Liability for loss and damage is the invoice value plus applicable paid freight." Our problem is that when our customer files a claim, the carrier insists on applying its tariff limitation of liability rather than the agreed-to contract value because we did not file the claim. Can they do this and how should we protect our customers and ourselves in the future?

A:

The legal issue is "what is the contract of carriage". The shipment was tendered to the carrier under your contract with the carrier.

Thus, the terms and conditions of the contract govern. Conversely, if there were no transportation agreement, the contract of carriage would be the bill of lading issued by the carrier to the shipper, and the tariffs, if any, incorporated therein by reference.

In the future, you could spell out in the contract what claims and liability provisions will apply to customer-filed claims. Note that terms of sale (such as FOB origin, FOB destination), which govern risk of loss in transit are of no concern to the carrier and are not binding on the carrier.

These terms are part of the contract of sale between seller and buyer and they are not part of the contract of carriage.

Contracts - Incorporation of Rate Tariffs

Q:

Some contract carriers are now stating that their discounts will be off the rates in effect on the date of shipment. Is this proper?

A:

In theory, the parties to a transportation contract can include any condition they wish to have govern the agreement. Remember, however that all of the terms and conditions are negotiable.

A properly drawn contract should state that the applicable rates and rules shall be those stated in the contract rather than those in the carrier's tariffs. If it is necessary to incorporate any portion of a carrier's tariff by reference, it should be limited to those

Provisions that are in effect on the date of the agreement. A copy of those tariff provisions should be attached to the contract. Anything less may subject the shipper to surprises.

Contracts - Released Rates on Computers

Q:

What are computer companies generally agreeing to in their contracts with motor carriers, $5.00 per lb. or higher?

A:

Sorry, we don't know what individual computer companies are doing in their contracts. Perhaps they will share that information with us, unless they have a confidentiality clause in their contracts.

Court Decisions on Carrier Liability

Q:

Where can I find recent court decisions on carrier liability?

A:

The Transportation Consumer Protection Council reports regularly on recent court decisions in its newsletter, Trans Digest. This is the best place to stay abreast of the latest developments.

TCPC also covers this type of information, in less extensive version.

Cross-Docking for Lower Rates

Q:

Can a shipper agree to cross-dock another shipper's freight to get a lower rate for the consolidated load, or would that require a broker's license?

A:

I see no reason why two shippers cannot do that without obtaining a license as a broker.

It would raise a question of how each shipper would be billed for 1/2 of the truckload rate, without subjecting one shipper to liability in the event one shipper failed to pay for its portion of the freight charges. Also consider liability exposure for personal injury and property damage during the cross-dock operation for the other shipper's freight.

Customer Chargebacks

Q:

We are having a lot of problems with unreasonable "chargebacks" from our customers. One example is "no packing lists on cartons". Such chargebacks can only be negotiated in the hope that the customer will be reasonable enough to realize that packing lists are sometimes torn off in transit. Aside from this, there is no way, short of videotaping each shipment as it leaves our dock, for a vendor to prove the packing lists were there. This is just one example. Do you have any suggestions?

A:

I can certainly sympathize with you about your chargeback problems. Unfortunately, there is not much you can do when dealing with a large, important customer that is in a position to dictate the terms and conditions which it includes in its purchase orders.

One thing that you should do is to carefully review customer purchase orders, and all of the terms and conditions which may be incorporated by reference, such as the customer's shipping instructions, routing guide, etc. If the chargebacks are not specifically set forth somewhere in your contractual agreement with the purchaser, you do not have to accept them. If you find unreasonable or offensive provisions, the time to correct them is during the negotiation phase, before you accept the purchase order and ship your goods. If the customer insists on including provisions which are unacceptable, you either have to live with them or refuse to sell your goods to that customer. I would suggest that you bring this to the attention of your top management and let them know what these practices are costing your company. Perhaps they would be in a better position to deal with their major customers' counterparts.

Damages - Missed Delivery Appointment

Q:

We use a common carrier to deliver our product. Recently, we had a job-site type delivery that the carrier had to perform.

On the bill of lading was a phone number for the carrier to contact. The carrier contacted the customer and made an appointment, the details or time of which were not know to us (the shipper).

The customer supposedly hired equipment to unload the shipment. The carrier was some two hours late, causing the customer to incur extra charges for the rental of equipment. The shipment was delivered and signed for clear . . . without exception.

Now the customer is withholding payment for our product, is back-charging us for the equipment rental, and wants us to file a claim against the carrier.

A:

You have two problems: one with your customer and one with the carrier.

The customer cannot withhold payment unless there is some contractual obligation which you have failed to perform. I would question whether there is anything in your purchase order, terms of sale, etc. which says anything about extra charges for late delivery, etc. Maybe that is where you should start.

In the absence of a special contract, the carrier is only required to deliver "with reasonable dispatch" and would not ordinarily be liable for a short delay of 2 hours. The carrier would undoubtedly deny your claim on the grounds that it is for "special damages" and they were not on notice that there would be extra charges for rental of equipment, etc. if they missed the appointment time.

Damages - Special Damages for Rail Service Failures

Q:

 It is my understanding that special damages claims could be filed against CSX and/or NS because of service failures due to the purchase of Conrail. Because of the poor service we have had to use truck service at a cost penalty to keep plants running. In addition, we lease a lot of rail cars that have sat idle due to the inability of the railroad to move equipment.

What documentation would be necessary to supply the railroad to support a special damages claim or is that decided by the railroad?

A:

Many shippers have experienced severe service problems since CSXT and Norfolk Southern took over operation of the former Conrail lines.

Although the Interstate Commerce Act requires rail carriers to provide "transportation or service on reasonable request", the legal obligation of these carriers to honor "special damage" claims for shipper's expenses resulting from service problems and delays is largely a function of the contracts and/or "circulars" which govern the traffic. However, in view of the embarrassing "meltdown" of the Union Pacific last year, and the public commitments of CSXT and Norfolk Southern, it is likely that these carriers will acknowledge their responsibility and make some reasonable compensation to affected shippers without the necessity for litigation.

In terms of documentation for "special damage" (delay) claims, I would suggest the following:

1. Review and analyze your historical transit times for movements between the same origins and destinations in order to determine the usual and normal transit times ("reasonable dispatch").

2. Save all communications (letters, e-mail, faxes, and memos of phone calls) to or from the carrier relating to problems in locating or tracing cars, misrouting, delays, delivery problems, etc. in order to show that the carrier had notice of the problems and the potential consequences of its service failures.

3. Document your damages with invoices, canceled checks, time sheets or other appropriate business records. Damages might include expenses of alternative transportation to meet delivery or production schedules, demurrage, detention, extra labor, overtime, higher prices for raw materials or parts purchased from other sources or vendors, administrative expenses, etc.

4. Be prepared to show how your damages were caused or necessitated by specific instances of delays or service failures.

Definitions - Logistics Company

Q:

What is a "Logistics Company"? Do they have to have any sort of broker license or authority?

A:

Many companies call themselves "logistics companies" today. They can be anything from a warehouse/distribution facility, a motor carrier, a freight forwarder, a broker, a shipper's agent, a consultant, or some combination of these functions. There is, unfortunately, no legal or official definition of a "logistics company."

Motor carriers, freight forwarders and property brokers are required by law to "register" with the FHWA and it is illegal to perform or provide these services without operating authority, insurance, surety bonds, etc. as provided in the Interstate Commerce Act and FHWA regulation. Unfortunately, the FHWA has limited resources to enforce the laws and many of them operate illegally.

You must be extremely careful when dealing with a "logistics company." Determine exactly what services are to be provided and demand copies of their operating authority, insurance, etc. before doing business. It is always advisable to enter into a written contract, which specifies the services, rates, rules, etc.

Definitions - Property Broker as Shipper

Q:

I sometimes see references to a "Dixie Midwest" decision in contract carriage agreements involving property brokers. Could you give me the definition of a shipper as stated in that decision and where could I get a copy of the document?

A:

The "Dixie Midwest" decision you refer to resulted from administrative appeals before the I.C.C. in which a number of motor carriers had applied for operating authority to provide service to brokers. The principal issues were whether a property broker can be considered a contract shipper, and, if so, the proper form of operating authority (common or contract).

The decision contains a lengthy discussion of the distinctions between "common" and "contract" carriage and the requirements for obtaining operating authority at that time (1982).

The I.C.C. essentially held that a property broker can be a contract shipper if he exercises sufficient control over the transportation, and meets certain criteria (payment of freight charges, regularity and continuity of traffic, specialized or particularized needs, etc.).

The decision may be found in 1982 Federal Carriers Cases, I would note that the ICC Termination Act of 1995 eliminated the statutory distinction between "common" and "contract" carriage. Thus, the issues which may have been relevant in 1982 are now essentially moot.

Detention Charges

Q:

What are the rules regarding a carrier billing for detention time? What paperwork is required for backup from the consignee and carrier? What is the time frame for figuring charge?

Appointment? Arrival? Start of unloading? Completion of unloading? Does the carrier have to provide written copies of rates with detention time listed to the consignee?

A:

I assume that you do not have a written transportation contract with the carrier. If you did, the contract would usually specify the rates, charges and rules applicable to your shipments, including detention charges, if any.

If you used a bill of lading which provides that it is subject to the carrier's tariffs, those tariffs are said to be "incorporated by reference" and become part of your contract. Detention charges are usually set forth in the carrier's "Rules Tariff". The rules tariff specifies the free time, when detention charges start to accrue, and how detention charges are calculated.

I would suggest the following:

If you are being billed for detention charges, demand a copy of the carrier's rules tariff. Carriers are required by law to provide copies of their tariffs upon demand by the shipper, you should not pay for detention.

In the future, you should enter into a properly drafted transportation contract with each of the carriers that you use.

If you are subject to detention charges, establish a company procedure for recording when equipment is placed or received, when notice is given to the carrier that the equipment is unloaded and available to be picked up, and when the equipment is actually picked up.

Discount Rates - Discounted from What?

Q:

Some contract carriers are now stating that their discounts will be off the rates in effect on the date of shipment. Is this proper?

A:

In theory, the parties to a transportation contract can include any condition they wish to have govern the agreement. Remember, however that all of the terms and conditions are negotiable.

A proper shipper-drawn contract should state that the rates and rules to apply shall be those stated in the contract, and not in the carrier's tariffs. If it is necessary to incorporate any portion of a carrier's tariff, it should only be those provisions that are in effect on the date of the agreement. A copy of those tariff provisions should be attached to the contract. Anything less may subject the shipper to surprises.

Duty to Accept Damaged Goods

Q:

We have a situation where a shipper loaded baled waste paper into a trailer and the load shifted in transit, causing the bales to fall over. Now the consignee refuses to accept the shipment and says he can't unload the bales because they would break apart. Doesn't the consignee have to accept the shipment?

A:

Normally, the consignee has a duty to accept a damaged shipment unless it is "substantially worthless", and also has a duty to take reasonable steps to mitigate damages.

In this case, it appears that the consignee can't remove the bales with his forklift equipment and could incur significant expense or other problems in trying to unload the truck. Since the fault is either with the shipper (for improper loading) or with the carrier (for causing the load shift), it does not seem that the consignee would be unreasonable in rejecting the load.

Factoring Companies

Q:

What can you tell me about "factoring companies" and how they fit in to the whole scheme of payment liabilities?

A:

Trucking companies often assign their accounts receivable to factoring companies or financial institutions. If you are notified by a factor that freight bills are to be paid to the factor, and not to the trucker, BEWARE!

First, this may be an indication that the motor carrier is in financial difficulty.

Second, you should double-check with BOTH the carrier and the factor to make sure that the accounts have actually been assigned. If you pay the wrong company you could be exposed to double payment liability.

Make sure you get confirmation IN WRITING.

FOB Terms vs. Payment Terms

Q:

I have a customer who claims that FOB terms (ownership of goods) and freight terms (burden of freight cost) are separate and that they could order from my company:

Freight - Prepaid

FOB Factory

Meaning that title would pass at my dock but the freight would be prepaid. Is this legal and/or correct?

A:

"FOB terms" are terms of sale and are defined in the Uniform Commercial Code. They govern the risk of loss in transit, i.e. whether the buyer or the seller has the risk in the event of loss or damage to the goods.

"Prepaid", "Collect" or "Bill to" terms are freight payment instructions which are generally entered on the bill of lading to tell the carrier which party should be sent the freight bill.

Thus, you can have a sale which is "FOB Origin", and the freight can be either prepaid, collect or bill to a third party.

Freezing of Perishables

Q:

The shipper marked the bill of lading "Perishable if frozen - prevent from freezing - take special precautions if weather deems necessary". Handwritten on the bill of lading, at the time of the pickup, was the notation, "trailer has no heat but has a team of drivers."

The carrier does not offer a heater service. However, the driver accepted the shipment and the shipment froze enroute. Is the carrier liable?

A:

In that case the carrier had a filed ICC tariff which said it would not accept shipments requiring protective service, and that shipments accepted which are subject to temperature damage are accepted only at the shipper's risk and responsibility. However, the court held that the Carmack Amendment prohibits a carrier from relying on such a tariff provision to exempt itself from liability once it accepts goods for transportation that require refrigeration. Since the bill of lading clearly put the carrier on notice of the perishable nature of the shipment, and the carrier accepted the shipment, I think the carrier is liable.

Freight Bills - Time Limits

Q:

I recently received over 100 invoices averaging $700 each, from a carrier who performed the pickup and delivery over a year ago. Some of the invoices are for services nearly two years ago. Is there a period of time within which the carrier must invoice for services rendered? And if not, is my company required to pay these within a certain length of time?

A:

Under the Interstate Commerce Act, a motor carrier must bring a civil action (lawsuit) to recover charges for transportation or service provided by the carrier within 18 months after the claim accrues. You have no legal obligation to pay freight bills after the expiration of the statute of limitations.

Freight Bills Received After 180 Days

Q:

Can freight companies collect on unpaid freight bills that are past the 180 day time limit? I have 5 bills from a company that they are saying have never been paid and I don't show them having been paid either. Are we responsible?

A:

Yes, freight companies can collect original, unpaid freight bills that are over 180 days old. The 180-day rule only applies when the carrier seeks to collect charges in addition to the original freight charges (i.e., freight undercharges). The only time limitation that would apply to the carrier's attempt to collect its original unpaid freight charges would be the 18 month statute of limitations.

Unless you have some other reason to dispute the unpaid bills, it would appear you are responsible for them.

Freight Charges - Billing to Customers

Q:

I am a volume shipper. As such I generally receive discounts from the carriers I use. Often these discounts fluctuate and, sometimes, the discount I receive is significantly larger than I anticipated in the pricing of my customer contracts. My standard sales bills contain separate charges for shipping. The shipping charge on the bill is what I anticipate the freight charge to be at the time of the order.

When I receive discounts greater than I anticipated, am I legally obliged to pass them on to my customers?

A:

Off bill discounting, essentially, this prohibited carriers from paying a discount or allowance to anyone other than the payor of the freight bill and required carriers to disclose all discounts or allowances on their freight bills. Neither the statutory provision nor the regulation are still in effect, due to subsequent legislation, namely the Trucking Industry Regulatory Reform Act of 1994 ("TIRRA") and the ICC Termination Act of 1995 ("ICCTA"). It should be noted that, in any event, the statutory provisions and regulations only applied to carriers, and not to shippers.

Thus, the real question is whether a purchaser could reasonably claim commercial fraud or misrepresentation if the seller adds an amount higher than the actual freight charge to its invoices.

Some companies place a notice, either in their terms of sale or on their invoices to disclose that the freight charges being invoiced do not reflect volume discounts or incentives received from the carrier. Others use wording such as "shipping and handling charge".

The best advice is to use a notice in your terms of sale and/or invoices which constitute a sufficient disclosure to your customer to avoid such claims.

Freight Charges - Broker Out of Business

Q:

I have recently read an article that someone had sent me regarding "double payment" in which you stated that this is a "gray area". My questions is how does a shipper get the collection agencies to stop bugging them? Let me take a minute and describe the situation. A shipper who had been doing business with a broker for well over 4 years has recently been notified by carriers that the broker has not paid them for freight do to the fact the broker has gone out of business and turn his affairs over to an attorney to handle his lack of monies to pay his freight bills. Now the broker was well established and had been in business for over 10 years and all of his authority and bond was in compliance at the time the freight shipped. Now the shipper obviously paid the broker as they have always did and the collection agencies are contacting the shipper for the money and these collections people are downright rude and harassing.

A:

Liability for freight charges depends on the facts and the relationships among the parties. Unfortunately, the "double payment" problem is very common when brokers go out of business or abscond with funds. This is a "gray area", and collection agencies and lawyers for the carriers will probably tell you that you are liable even though you have paid the broker.

However, the general rule, as supported by a number of court decisions, is that if the shipper has dealt only with the broker, and has paid the broker, the carrier cannot come back to the shipper to collect its freight charges. The legal rationale is that there is no privity of contract between the shipper and the carrier; also, that the carrier has extended credit to the broker, and not to the shipper.

There is not much you can do when being harassed by collection agencies or lawyers, other than to tell them - very firmly - that you have no intention of paying them, because you have already paid the broker

Freight Charges - Shipper Liability to Subcontractor

Q:

Is a shipper liable to a truck line for freight charges owed to it by a steamship line when the ocean carrier issued a through door-to-door bill of lading, hired the truck line for the inland move, and collected freight charges from the shipper, but failed to pay the trucker?

A:

No. Under a through Bill of Lading, the shipper's contract is with the ocean carrier, and there is no privity of contract between the trucker and shipper. We note, however, a growing number of these occurrences due to the slow pay cycles occurring in the ocean trade.

Freight Charges - Shippers Liability

Q:

I have a manufacturing client who shipped goods freight collect (clearly indicated on bill of lading and signed by carrier) to a consignee who later went bankrupt and didn't pay the freight bills. Now the carrier is coming back to the shipper for payment. I have many of your books, but I could not find information directly on point. I found information regarding brokers and freight forwarders, but not bankrupt consignees.

A:

It appears that you do not have any written transportation contract with the carrier in question, and that the shipment moved in common carriage under a standard bill of lading.

A shipper will remain liable for freight charges even if the bill of lading is marked "collect", UNLESS the shipper executes the "non-recourse" or "Section 7" box on the face of the bill of lading. The non-recourse provision will generally protect the shipper if the consignee fails to pay or goes bankrupt.

Freight Charges - Shipper's Liability; "Section 7"

Q:

If a carrier agrees to deliver freight to a customer on a collect basis and the consignee goes out of business before paying the freight charges, who is then responsible for paying the freight charges?

A:

The general rule is that the shipper is primarily liable for payment of freight charges. A shipper may be able to protect himself on a collect shipment by signing what is referred to as the "non-recourse" or "Section 7" provision - a box on the front of the uniform straight bill of lading. Unless this is done, however, and the consignee fails to pay, the carrier can go back to the shipper for payment.

Freight Charges - Statute of Limitations

Q:

What is the applicable statute of limitations for a trucking company to collect freight charges, when the shipper paid the broker and the broker went "belly up" and never paid the trucker? The trucker says it is the 5 years, which is the statute of limitations in our state. The shipments in question moved from New York to Nebraska.

A:

The applicable statute of limitations is the 18 month time limit, prior to the ICC Termination Act, there were other statutes of limitation in effect, for many years the statute of limitations was 3 years; it was shortened by the Negotiated Rates Act of 1993 in two phases - first to 2 years, then to 18 months.

Note: The only exception that comes to mind is if the carrier was acting as a contract carrier (as opposed to a common carrier) in which case the parties could have included some other time limit for bringing suit in their contract.

I would also observe that there is a body of case law which supports the position that a shipper which has paid a broker cannot be liable ("double payment") to the motor carrier.

Freight Forwarders - Legal Requirements

Q:

I am starting a freight forwarding business and was wondering what laws apply to international and domestic freight forwarding?

A:

There are laws, but it depends on what you are planning to do.

- Domestic surface freight forwarders are required to register with the FHWA and must file evidence of insurance and registered agents for service of process.

- Ocean freight forwarders are regulated by the FMC and must be licensed and bonded.

- Air freight forwarders are not regulated by any government agency.

Holding Freight for "Ransom"

Q:

We are a freight forwarder that periodically has had a vendor or supplier hold our freight as ransom in order to have past due debts paid, or to collect COD shipments. Is this legal, and can we recover our freight from off their dock, even if we prepaid for the shipment?

A:

From the information in your memo, it is not clear what the problem is, particularly what you mean by "our freight". As a freight forwarder, you normally have no ownership interest in the goods.

Assuming you are talking about your line-haul carriers holding freight or refusing to deliver because you owe them freight charges, carriers have a lien for freight charges on shipments they are transporting, and can lawfully refuse to deliver until the freight charges are paid. It should be noted that in most states, the lien only applies to the current shipment being transported, and not to freight charges on past shipments. In California, however, the law permits carriers to hold freight for all past freight charges.

Household Goods - Estimates

Q:

Is there any remedy when a HHG "estimate" is exceeded by 50% when the actual weight is calculated and used to calculate the freight charges?

A:

Your only remedy is to pay the estimated freight charge plus 10% to obtain delivery of your belongings and then to contest the balance. If the shipper did not receive a "binding estimate", or competitive bids, you are at the mercy of the carrier.

One of the recurring problems with estimates is "low balling" the estimate to get the contract, and then charging for the actual weight. Another problem has been "ballooning" the weight when the truck is placed on the scale.

Therefore, if other bids are obtained, at least they may be used to contest the actual weight and freight bill.

ICCTA - Clarification

Q:

Could you provide some clarification on the acronym ICCTA? What does it stands for? Of what relevance is it to the average citizen consumer?

A:

"ICCTA" stands for the ICC Termination Act of 1995, which was effective on January 1, 1996. This was the most recent legislation intended to deregulate the trucking industry which started with the Motor Carrier Act of 1980, followed by the Negotiated Rates Act of 1993, the Trucking Industry Regulatory Reform Act of 1994, and the Federal Aviation Administration Act of 1994 (which deregulated intrastate trucking).

ICCTA abolished the ICC and transferred the remaining functions to the Department of Transportation (FHWA or Surface Transportation Board). It also re-codified the Interstate Commerce Act, and incorporated or modified provisions or the earlier legislation.

Improper Loading - Act of Shipper

Q:

We recently shipped a machine from Portland to Memphis. The machine was professionally loaded into the trailer by licensed machinery movers. The driver slept thru the process, and then left to get a meal. The dock area is on the side of our building and open to the public. The load was additionally insured. The driver closed up the trailer.

The machine was damaged extensively. The trucking company is denying any liability saying that the driver was denied access to the trailer during the loading and therefore implies that all damage was ours due to inappropriate loading. We strongly disagree.

What should we do?

A:

The legal principles are fairly straight-forward: the claimant has the burden of proving that the machine was tendered to the carrier in good order and condition, and arrived in damaged condition.

The carrier has the burden of proving that the sole and proximate cause of the damage was one of the "excepted causes" - in this case an "act of the shipper" - improper loading, blocking or bracing.

Whether the driver participated in the loading or not, it appears he did have the opportunity to witness the loading. In addition, Federal Highway Administration regulations place a duty on the driver to make sure cargo is properly secured, last, but not least, if the machine was not properly loaded or secured, the driver should have refused to accept it.

Since you apparently hired a rigging company to load the machine, I would suggest that you get a detailed written statement from the people who did the actual loading, together with any loading diagrams, photos, etc. that may exist, and submit these with the claim.

Insurance Requirements - Courier & Messenger Services

Q:

What insurance requirement do couriers and messenger service carriers have today?

A:

Most local courier and messenger services only operate within an exempt commercial zone and, as such are not subject to federal requirements governing interstate for-hire motor carriers. If they do operate trucks in interstate commerce they would be required to register with the FHWA, and would be subject to regulations requiring public liability and cargo insurance, including the BMC 32 cargo endorsement.

Interstate vs. Intrastate

Q:

As the office manager of a small interstate contract for-hire carrier, I have the following question. We have received a citation from the Pennsylvania PUC., for picking up and delivering within the state of PA. The problem is that this was not an INTRASTATE movement. The load was loaded thru a freight forwarding company at Atglen, PA and the load had 7 stops in PA, 1 stop in NY and a final with 2 stops in OH (our home state). What law or regulation covers this type of movement (picking up in one state with intermediate deliveries in the same state but with a final delivery in another state, all from the same shipper).

A:

There are no "regulations", but there is a section of the Interstate Commerce Act which essentially defines Interstate Commerce as it applies to the regulation of motor carriers, under that definition and the relevant court decisions, the movement you described would be considered "interstate" in character.

Late Payment Charges

Q:

We have recently been contacted by a trucking company on a small number of invoices that we paid on an over 60 day's basis. They are trying to eliminate our discount on these old and paid invoices because they were paid late.

Are these claims valid?

A:

First, I am not surprised that other carriers are starting to press to collect their late payment penalties in view of the recent decision in Humboldt Express v. The Wise Co. (which is on appeal to the 4th Circuit Court of Appeals, by the way).

Whether late payment penalties are enforceable depends on a number of factors including whether the carrier complied with the ICC's credit regulations, whether there was a proper notice on the original freight bills, etc. There is also the question of whether the late payment charges are an unreasonable penalty of forfeiture. Usually, each case must be evaluated on its own particular set of facts. I would advise you to consult an experienced transportation attorney.

Liability - Carrier's Liability on Refused Shipments

Q:

This question applies primarily to LTL transportation. Regarding storage on refused shipments, I have been unable to find anything in the NMFC rules that sets time limits on when a carrier can begin charging storage on refused shipments. Depending on the carrier and the business volume associated with a specific carrier, the rules change. Since I handle multiple shipping locations, I am trying to get some consistency in our

OS&D program and would like to know if there are any rules governing storage and the carrier's obligation to notify the shipper (mode of notification) on refused shipments.

A:

Assuming that you are shipping by common carrier under a Uniform Straight Bill of Lading, the relevant provisions are found in Section 4 of the terms and conditions on the reverse side of the bill of lading. This section provides:

If the consignee refuses the shipment... the carrier's liability shall then become that of a warehouseman.

Carrier shall promptly attempt to provide notice...to the shipper of party, if any, designated to receive notice on this bill of lading.... Storage charges, based on the carrier's tariff, shall start no sooner than the next business day following the attempted notification...

In other words, the Uniform Straight Bill of Lading essentially defers to the individual carrier's tariff for details as to storage rates and rules.

This is one of the reasons why shippers must always be careful to demand a copy of the carrier's rules tariff before doing business, since these tariffs contain the rules governing storage charges (as well as other rules governing accessorial charges, credit terms, liability limitations, etc.).

I would point out that the problems you discuss can be obviated by a properly drafted Transportation Contract, and we always recommend that our clients use such contracts with their motor carriers.

Liability - Custom Order Goods

Q:

A custom order that we shipped was partially damaged and the consignee refused delivery because the product could not be used. Because this was a custom order, there is no salvage value so we filed a claim for the full amount, which was declined by the carrier on the basis that it was not on notice of the nature of the goods. What is our recourse?

A:

By basing its declination on lack of notice of the nature of the goods, it appears the carrier is declining this claim on the basis that you are seeking "special damages". However, this is incorrect and damage to a shipment which consists of something specially made for a consignee would be characterized as general damage making the carrier liable for its full invoice value less any salvage value. The fact that the shipment was specially designed does not transform the damages into special damages.

Liability - Limitation When Broker Involved

Q:

We used a broker to move an interstate shipment in January 2013. The item was damaged beyond repair by the carrier. We filed our written claim February 23rd.

Finally today we were advised the carrier will issue a check based on their coverage terms on their Bill of Lading which is $0.50 per lb. or $50.00, whichever is greater.

We were not made aware of these terms by the broker we used. The reimbursement comes to 20% of the product value.

We are bound by the carrier's clause on their Bill of Lading as noted above or is the carrier responsible to pay in full the invoice value of the item they broke? What are our options/recourses?

A:

Your experience illustrates one of the dangers of using brokers to arrange transportation on your behalf. It would appear that your broker may have used a carrier which had a limitation of liability either in its bill of lading or a tariff which was incorporated by reference through the bill of lading.

If you have a written contract with your broker or have otherwise made it clear that the broker is only to ship at full liability, and may not agree to released rates or limited liability, you may have a claim against the broker. If this requirement was not made clear to the broker, it could be argued that he had the authority to agree to limited liability in return for a cheap freight rate.

Whether the motor carrier can enforce a limitation of liability is another question. This depends on the bill of lading that was used, whether there was adequate notice of the limitation of liability, whether there was a choice of full vs. limited liability, and whether the carrier maintained a proper tariff containing the liability limitation. If the amount in dispute is significant, I would certainly recommend that you have a qualified transportation attorney review the file to determine if the carrier can lawfully enforce its limitation of liability. In other words, don't take "no" for an answer.

Liability as a Rate Factor

Q:

We have witnessed carriers setting liability limits on our freight, which they could not previously publish. Can we now force the National Classification Committee to drop liability as a factor in classifying our freight?

A:

Good thought, as the carriers are not offering a reduction in rates as a quid pro quo for the reduction in liability. Shippers should use this argument to oppose new liability limitations proposed by their carriers. It would be a waste of time and effort to suggest that liability be dropped as a classification factor as shippers have no real or effective vote on the Classification Committee, which may be going out of existence soon.

Liability for Stolen Freight - Carrier's Terminal

Q:

Is a carrier liable for goods stolen from it while they were being held after rejection by the consignee? They were stolen from the carrier's terminal which had no alarm, no security, but the pin lock was broken and the trailer stolen.

A:

With goods being held after rejection, the carrier's liability is that of a warehouseman. It is then liable only for negligence, as it must exercise reasonable care such as that of a reasonably prudent person caring for his own goods.

Therefore, the question is whether a prudent person would have had an alarm and security guards in that particular location to protect his own goods.

Liability on Sealed Container Shortage

Q:

I have a situation where I am not sure who is at fault. I have a vendor that had the driver, when picking up a rail container, sign it "Shipper Load, Driver Count." The container was sealed at the pickup point with the driver in attendance and the above notation then placed on the Original Bill of Lading. When delivered we cut the seal (same number) and unloaded the trailer without assist. Our dock man came up 40 cartons short. Against whom do we, as the consignee, have a claim?

I am not sure if we file against the vendor or the carrier that picked up the container.

A:

Obviously, you have a mystery on your hands.

Ordinarily, "shipper load, driver count" would shift responsibility to the carrier for any shortage discovered upon delivery at destination.

However, when the container is sealed, and if the original seal is intact at destination, it is strong evidence that the shortage could not have occurred in transit. There are cases where seals have been tampered with - opened up and re-attached, or glued back with "crazy glue", etc., and where door hinges have been removed without breaking the seals, but I assume you made a thorough inspection of the container and ruled out such possibilities.

My suggestion would be to talk to the shipper and ask for independent verification that the goods were actually loaded. Ask for their loading records or a stroke tally, and have them check their inventory to see if the goods may still be in the warehouse. If you are satisfied that the goods were loaded into the container, and feel that you can prove this to the carrier, then file your claim with the carrier.

Lastly, check your terms of sale. If the shipment was "FOB Origin", the risk of loss would be on the buyer (consignee); if the shipment was "FOB Destination", the risk of loss would be on the seller (shipper).

Limitation of Liability - No Bill of Lading

Q:

A carrier picks up a shipment but fails to issue a bill of lading. The shipment is damaged in transit. The carrier claims that its liability is limited to $50/load because the shipper did not declare a value on the bill of lading. Can the carrier enforce its limited liability provision?

A:

No. It is the carrier's responsibility to issue a bill of lading. Because the carrier failed to issue the bill of lading the shipper had no notice of the terms of the bill of lading and thus had no opportunity to declare a value.

Loading and Unloading - Driver Injuries

Q:

We are a large concrete accessories manufacturer and in 2013 we shipped some construction materials to a job site through a broker.

The driver working for the broker decided to assist in unloading the product when he arrived at the site without our request to do so. He injured himself and he is now waiving his rights to workman's compensation and is suing the broker and my company instead. We did not have a specific contract with the broker at the time (our mistake), so I believe that there is not a hold harmless clause to protect us. Where does our legal liability end in such a situation?

A:

This is not a simple question. There are dozens of reported court decisions involving liability for "loading and unloading" accidents. Many of these involve interpretation of insurance policies and various state laws, and often the cases are very fact-specific. A formal opinion as to your company's liability would require thorough analysis of the facts, research into applicable state law, etc.

I assume that your company has appropriate general liability coverage, and that this matter has been turned over to your insurance company for the legal defense of the lawsuit. If not, this should be done promptly.

Regarding contracts with brokers or motor carriers, we strongly recommend that shippers use properly drafted transportation agreements. Such agreements may contain provisions for indemnification, which would be helpful protection in situations such as you have described.

Lumping Fees

Q:

What should we do when we encounter receivers who require the trucker to pay unloading fees without any compensation to the truck operator? Doesn't the Interstate Commerce Act prohibit this?

A:

Yes, section 14103 of the Interstate Commerce Act prohibits "lumping." This section provides that if the shipper or receiver requires a carrier to be assisted in loading or unloading a truck, the shipper or receiver must either provide the assistance or compensate the carrier for the cost. This is a federal statute and violation is a federal crime.

While there is no guarantee of a response, it is recommended that you report violations to the Federal Highway Administration and ask them to enforce the law. Try writing to them at: Federal Highway Administration.

Measure of Damages - Limits & Consequential Damages

Q:

We recently purchased a used blueprint machine and had it shipped via common carrier to our business. When it arrived, on a pallet with 'Fragile' markings, the machine packaging was torn up. Upon inspection we found concealed damage.

We called a local company to repair the damage, noting the $25.00 per pound allowance on the freight bill. The final repair cost was less than $25/lb., but more than the value of the machine.

The carrier does not want to pay more than the value of the equipment, but we have found Rule 600 paragraph (A) of the Interstate Commerce Act that states 'carriers are liable for the full actual loss, damage or injury actually caused by such carriers while property is in their care...'.

This is not like a car, where a total loss can get you a similar one of the same value. This machine is hard to find. We also needed the machine the day it arrived, and could not wait for a replacement.

Who is right?

A:

First of all, you should understand that the $25.00 per pound is a "limitation of liability"; if properly set forth in the carrier's bill of lading and/or tariffs, it would be a maximum amount the carrier would have to pay.

Second, there is a general principle that a shipper or consignee has a duty to "mitigate" the loss. Normally this means that you should not spend more to repair a damaged item than it would cost to purchase a replacement unit.

Third, the usual measure of damages - as set forth in the court decisions - is "destination market value". Usually this is established by the invoice price from the seller plus the freight charges. However, there are exceptions to this general rule and there are cases in which a consignee of a shipment is entitled to the cost to replace a lost or damaged item.

In your case, you suggest that you were unable to purchase a replacement from the original vendor.

This raises the question as to what it would have cost to buy a replacement locally (or somewhere else and have it shipped to you). What I would suggest is that you obtain quotes for a similar used machine, and if they are more than what you spent to repair the machine, submit them to the carrier as evidence of the replacement value.

Lastly, there may be an issue of what is called "special or consequential damages". You indicate that you could not wait for a replacement and had to have it repaired the same day. The carrier is not responsible for any additional damages (over the value of the property lost or damaged) unless it has some actual or constructive notice, at the time of shipment, that such damages may be incurred. In other words, if the carrier did not know that you had an immediate need for the machine, it should not have to pay for the amount which the cost of repair exceeded the replacement value.

Measure of Damages - Released Rate Shipment

Q:

When we released a shipment of pharmaceuticals at $2.00 per lb. and the shipment is stolen, are we entitled to the invoice value, or only $2.00 per lb., or as the carrier's insurance company claims, only our manufactured costs?

A:

You are entitled to recover based on your invoice value if the goods had been sold, and were stolen while in transit to a customer. However, in most cases it doesn't matter whether invoice value or manufactured cost is used. If there is a valid limitation of liability, the most you can collect is $2.00 per lb. times the weight of the shipment.

Measure of Damages - Repair Cost

Q:

We purchased a used machine that is hard to find, but it was damaged en route. As we needed it the day it arrived, we were forced to have it repaired the same day. The repair cost was greater than the cost of the machine, but less than the carrier's $25 per lb. limit. Are we entitled to recover the repair cost?

A:

If you can obtain quotations for the cost of the same machine, use them as evidence of the replacement value, for cases on the market value, including replacement costs.

Measure of Damages - Return Shipment

Q:

We filed a claim against a carrier for the full invoice value of a shipment that they (the carrier) had lost. The carrier offered the shipment for delivery but the consignee refused it because the purchase order was cancelled.

Disposition was issued to the carrier to return the merchandise. Subsequently. The goods were lost by the carrier.

The carrier, while admitting liability, claims that the proper measure of loss should be the manufactured cost of goods.

Their reasoning is that, since the shipment was refused by the consignee, there was no longer a consummated sale. Once there was no sale, the argue, the value of the goods reverted to manufactured cost.

A:

This is an interesting fact pattern, and I am not aware of any decisions directly on point.

The usual measure of damages is the "destination market value" and this is most often established by using the invoice price to the customer. However, since the P.O. was canceled (and the invoice also), the case falls more closely into the rationale of the Polaroid and Kodak cases (warehouse to warehouse movements), these cases essentially say that the claimant is entitled to its selling price (less expenses not incurred) because the goods would have been sold within a short time.

I am attaching a memo which was recently provided to another client on a similar claim.

As I understand it, your customer returned goods for which Square D agreed to give a credit of the original invoice value. The goods were lost or damaged en route and you filed a claim based on the invoice value. The carrier has denied the claim and argues that the measure of damages is your inventory cost.

I am not aware of a case factually on point, but the closest analogy would the "warehouse-to-warehouse" situation in Polaroid Corp. v. Shusters Express, Inc., where the court stated:

The fact that the plaintiff was transporting goods to its own warehouse and not to a buyer does not change the measure of damages. The affidavits established a more than reasonable likelihood that the hijacked goods would have been sold at the claimed market price.

The reasoning in Polaroid has been adopted in Eastman Kodak Co. v. Westway Motor Freight, Inc, In Eastman Kodak, the Tenth Circuit held that the defendant had not sufficiently established "special reasons" for departing from the market value rule. The court noted that, "Kodak produced evidence that it sells virtually all of its sensitized photographic merchandise shortly after production is completed. This evidence tends to show that any damaged merchandise that could not be sold would result in lost profits." The court thus held that the full invoice (wholesale) price was the correct measure of damages since the carrier presented no evidence that the merchandise would have been sold at a lower price.

The Burton case also makes it clear that where a carrier asserts that some other measure of damages should be used (such as "replacement cost"), the carrier would have the burden of proving that the shipper did not lose any sales:

On the remand Preston, as the carrier, will have the burden of proof to demonstrate that its loss of the 81 cases of cigarette papers did not cause Burton any loss of sales. ...But, if Preston cannot establish that Burton did not lose any sales by reason of the loss of the goods, the district court will enter judgment against Preston for $55,928.99, the invoice price. If the district court finds that Burton lost sales by reason of the loss of the merchandise it should not attempt to quantify the inherently uncertain amount of the loss. Thus, unless Preston establishes that Burton did not lose any sales by reason of the loss of the 81 cases of cigarette papers, it will not have demonstrated that the court should deviate from the market value rule.

Measure of Damages - Return Shipment

Q:

When freight is refused from the carrier because the purchase order was cancelled, the carrier wants our claim to be amended to reflect "manufactured cost" because there was no longer a consummated sale.

A:

The Polaroid and Kodak cases discussed therein hold that if you can establish that the goods would have been sold within a short period of time (usually by introducing records of storage turnover rates for the products involved), you are entitled to the invoice value, not merely manufactured costs.

Notice of Claim - Rail Shipments

Q:

We are having a problem with railroads declining claims because they were not notified of the damage or shortage within 24 hours of delivery. This seems unrealistic. Is it legal?

A:

While this seems unreasonable, it is probably enforceable if the 24-hour notice requirement is part of your contract or is included in the railroad's Exempt Circular.

However, liability conditions such as this can and should be negotiated out of the agreement at its inception. There are also many other unreasonable rules in railroad contracts and Exempt Circulars that you can be bound by, so it is imperative that any agreement with the railroad be reviewed and revised as appropriate.

Notice of Refused or On-Hand Freight

Q:

When a Bill of Lading instructs the carrier to bill a third party, and the shipment is refused by the consignee, who should the carrier notify, the consignor (shipper) or the third party?

A:

Section 4. (a) 1. Of the Uniform Straight Bill of Lading requires the carrier to attempt to provide notice to "the shipper or the party, if any, designated to receive notice" on the bill of lading. It does not require the carrier to notify a party merely designated as the "bill to" party.

On the other hand, since the carrier was placed on notice that a third party had an interest in the shipment, it would be reasonable to assume the carrier should have some obligation to send a copy of the notice to that party.

This question illustrates the benefit of having a formal transportation agreement which clearly spells out the obligations of the parties.

NVOCC'S and Ocean Freight Forwarders

Q:

What is an "NVOCC" and how is it different from an ocean freight forwarder?

A:

Prior to the Ocean Shipping Reform Act, an "NVOCC" (non-vessel-operating common carrier) was defined as "a common carrier that does not operate the vessel8s by which the ocean transportation is provided, and is a shipper in its relationship with an ocean common carrier".

Typically, NVOCC's consolidate less-than-container shipments into full container loads, which are then tendered to the ocean carrier. The NVOCC issues bills of lading to its shippers, and is liable to the shipper for loss or damage in transit. Rates and charges were required to be filed in tariff form with the FMC.

Ocean freight forwarders, on the other hand, were not carriers. Ocean freight forwarders were defined as "a person in the United States that: (1) Dispatches shipments from the United States via common carriers and books or otherwise arranges space for those shipments on behalf of shippers; and (2) Processes the documentation or performs related activities incident to those shipments".

Forwarders act as agents of the shipper, prepare documentation, make shipping and insurance arrangements, handle billings and payments, etc.

The Ocean Shipping Reform Act created a new category of "Ocean Transportation Intermediaries" or "OTI's" which includes both NVOCC's and ocean freight forwarders.

OTI's are required to be licensed by the Federal Maritime Commission, and are required to file surety bonds. The FMC regulations continue to distinguish between an OTI that performs "NVOCC' functions and one that only performs "freight forwarder" functions. It may be noted that, in countries other than the U.S., there is usually no distinction between an NVOCC and a forwarder, and forwarders often perform the functions of both.

Offsetting Claims against Freight Charges

Q:

Where does the law prohibit a shipper from deducting claims from freight charges owed to a carrier?

A:

It doesn't. At one time carriers were prohibited from offsetting claims against freight charges on the grounds that it could result in discrimination among their customers. However, the anti-discrimination statute was repealed in ICCTA

However, before offsetting claims, a shipper should check the carrier's tariff rules for penalties, such as a loss-of-discount, for failure to pay freight charges within a specific time, some carriers prohibit offsetting in their rules tariff. Shippers can negotiate to waive these rules, and contract shippers can insert appropriate provisions in their contracts.

Overcharge Claims - A Solution to the 180-Day Rule?

Q:

 As new members of TCPC, we were wondering if you could please tell us if the below statement made at the time of freight bill payment legally fulfills the requirements of the 180-Day Rule?

"In compliance with Public, we hereby contest all freight charges being billed and paid on the below listed invoices and, thus fulfill the requirements of the 180-Day Rule."

If so, we would recommend that a shipper make this statement at the time of freight bill payment by way of an attachment to the check, a check stub statement or even a stamp reading this way on each paid freight bill.

Please let us know your opinion of this strategy to extend the statute for the filing of overcharge claims.

A:

Your suggested procedure is novel, but it should work. There is no specific procedure to "contest" freight bills set. I don't see any difference between your form of notice and the notices that carriers often print on the back of their freight bills or invoices.

Refused or Rejected Freight

Q:

What happens with freight collect shipments that are refused by the consignee? (The refusals were not related to damages.) It is my belief that, once abandoned, the carrier would dispose of the goods through sale or auction of some sort.

A:

I think you have correctly evaluated the situation. The carrier has certain responsibilities when a shipment is refused or can't be delivered. It must use reasonable efforts to protect the property, notify the shipper and owner that the goods are on hand, etc.

The carrier has a lien for its freight charges, and can sell the goods to pay its lien, provided that certain procedures are followed. If the goods are sold, the proceeds would then be first used to offset the original outbound freight charges and pay any expenses associated with the sale. If the sale did not generate enough revenue to cover the freight and expenses, the balance would be billed to the shipper.

If the freight and expenses were fully paid from the sale revenue, the balance should be sent to the shipper.

Take a look at Section 4(a) of the contract terms and conditions on the reverse side of the Uniform Straight Bill of Lading.

Remedies - Carrier Holding Freight Hostage

Q:

We have had some disputes with a trucker over freight bills. We found he was overcharging based on his tariff, and cut the bills back to the proper rate. Yesterday we gave him a shipment, and now he is holding the shipment "hostage" for the total amount that he claims is due (about $3,700). The freight for this particular shipment is only $360. Can he do this?

A:

Carriers have a "carrier's lien" on any shipment they are transporting, but only for the freight charges relating to the shipment in their possession, and not for previous shipments. If you tender the $360 for the freight charges on this shipment, the carrier legally must release the shipment. If he doesn't, he will be "converting" your property and you have a remedy in court.

Responsibility for Consequential Damages

Q:

I am the Assistant Manager of an automotive component manufacturer with numerous facilities. We are a major "tier one" supplier for the Big Three in North America, Canada & Mexico. We also supply parts to most of the North American automotive transplant operations as well as various automotive joint venture operations.

We are currently in a very delicate position with one of our customers located in Canada. Our terms of sale with this customer are "F.O.B. DESTINATION" but the transportation system is controlled by this customer and they pay all transportation costs.

In January, we were notified by the customer that we had short-shipped on a previous shipment and that we needed to make an expedited shipment to prevent a line shut-down. In order to make the delivery before their line shut-down, our only option was to arrange an air charter from our Missouri plant to Canada.

We immediately began making such arrangements and everything was in place to get the parts to Ontario airport by 2:00 p.m. that same day. When we contacted our customer to inform them of our arrangements and make a delivery appointment, the customer instructed us to cease our efforts. They informed us that they wanted their carrier to handle this expedited delivery.

They instructed us to arrange for an expedited carrier to pick up the shipment, take it to their carrier's consolidation facility in Ohio. We were informed that their carrier would arrange the air charter from their consolidation point in Ohio to Canada. Since this customer normally controls and arranges the transportation, we consented to their direction for this shipment also.

The expedited carrier picked the shipment up from our facility and took it to their consolidation location in Ohio where is was put on a truck, not an airplane, for delivery to Canada. Needless to say, the truck did not make it to the plant in time to prevent the line shut-down.

Now the customer is attempting to hold us responsible for $20K in down-time expenses for the "delivery failure."

We are contending that we should not be held responsible because we were not in control of the transportation arrangements. Had we been in control, the shipment would have arrived at their location several hours before the stated shut-down time.

The customer is alleging that because the terms are "F.O.B. DESTINATION", we are liable for these charges. I am arguing that the F.O.B. point is irrelevant in this situation because the parts themselves were undamaged and in acceptable condition at time of delivery. It was their delivery system which failed and caused the line shut-down. Our parts did not cause this line shut-down.

As far as a contract between our company and this customer, one does not exist to my knowledge. I am trying to get a copy of this customer's Purchase Order to us to see if it addresses the issue of consequential damages, but my initial guess is, no such issues are addressed.

I feel that this customer is being directed by their carrier to hold us responsible because the carrier doesn't want to be held responsible.

I believe that if we could present the opinion of a "recognized authority" in matters such as these to the customer, the customer would be able to see where the responsibility for the failure truly lies.

A:

I will attempt to reply based on your description of the facts.

First, there are two separate contracts involved: (1) between buyer and seller, and (2) between shipper and carrier.

The first contract appears to be a "just in time" arrangement between a supplier and its customer, although you indicate that there is no written contract between the parties. As to the purchase order, it would be helpful to have a copy to review in order to determine what (if any) provisions cover delays or late deliveries.

The "terms of sale" (FOB Destination) which you refer to generally relate to risk of loss in transit, i.e., loss or damage to the property while in the hands of a carrier. If the terms of sale are FOB Destination, under UCC 2-319, there is a presumption that the seller has risk of loss in transit. However, I do not see how this provision of the UCC would have any bearing on your customer's claim for consequential damages.

It would be my opinion, (in the absence of contrary provisions in the JIT contract or the purchaser order) that your customer, by having made the transportation arrangements with its own carrier, assumed responsibility for any delay resulting from the use of that carrier.

The second contract is between shipper and carrier and is subject to principles of transportation law, e.g. the "Carmack Amendment", etc. As to a possible claim against the trucker, a claim for "down time" resulting from delay is a classic example of "special damages". Special damages are recoverable from a carrier only if there is actual or constructive notice, at the time of shipment, of the consequences of delay or non-delivery. If the carrier was on notice of the urgency of this shipment and that delay would cause a plant shutdown, it is possible that the carrier could be held liable.

From what you have told me, I would suggest that your customer should pursue its claim for damages against the carrier, and not against your company.

Retention of Bills of Lading and Similar Documents

Q:

How long should shippers keep bills of lading, freight bills, etc?

A:

Bills of lading and freight bills may be important if you have a dispute with a carrier over freight charges, or if the carrier goes bankrupt and its "auditors" try to assert claims for undercharges or late payment penalties. The time limit in the Interstate Commerce Act for a carrier to bring an action for freight charges is now 18 months. However, under the Bankruptcy Act, statutes of limitation are extended by 2 years from the date the petition in bankruptcy is filed. Thus, to be safe, you should probably hang on to these records and documents for a minimum of 3 1/2 years.

Also, if you have a loss and damage claim pending for a long period of time, you should keep all files on that shipment until it is closed. You will need those files to establish good condition at origin, invoice prices, sales contracts, quality control documents, loading diagrams, etc. in the event of trial. These records should be kept for at least two years after declination of the claim if you intend to institute suit within that period.

Retention of Shipping Documents

Q:

In light of the most recent changes to the Interstate Commerce Act, what period of time do you recommend we use for shipping document retention? We want to direct a uniform document retention plan for our Distribution Centers.

A:

Unlike carriers, who are required by the Code of Federal Regulations (CFR) to maintain certain documents for various periods of time (49 CFR §379), there are no similar provisions for shippers. Therefore, we generally recommend that freight bills and bills of lading are retained for a minimum of 3 1/2 years. The reasoning is that the statute of limitations on recovery of freight charges by a carrier is now 18 months and statutes of limitation can be extended by 2 years if a carrier files for bankruptcy. Note that this recommendation does NOT take into account any record retention requirements that might be imposed by the IRS, SEC, other federal, state or local jurisdictions or other regulatory agencies.

Return of Damaged Goods

Q:

Could you please comment on carrier responsibility for return of damaged goods?

I ship regularly with a specific carrier and have experienced some minimal damages. The problem is that, due to the nature of our product, it must be returned to our facility for verified disposal. My question is related to the return of damaged product.

Who is responsible to pay for the return of damaged goods to my facility?

The carrier has, until now, been returning the product on a free astray basis. They have recently informed me that, since I am filing claims on this damaged and unusable product, I am responsible for the cost of returning the product to our facility. I disagree.

It seems to me that since THEY damaged the product, THEY should be responsible, not only for the cost of the damaged goods, but also for any related costs incurred as a result of this damage. In my view, due to the necessity of disposal at our facility, they are responsible for the free astray return of the goods.

If they do decide to "charge" me for the return transportation, am I within my rights to include those charges in my claim.

A:

There are no "black and white" answers when you get into the area of measure of damages for a loss and damage claim. However, let's start with the concept that you have a duty to mitigate damages. This means that reasonable costs and expenses to sort, segregate, inspect, repair, etc. are part of your damages and thus includable in your claim. If damaged goods have to be brought back to your facility as part of the salvage procedure, any freight charges for the return of the goods should be a legitimate element of damages. (As you note, many carriers handle this on a "free astray" basis without any charge.)

Risk of Loss in Transit

Q:

Our company purchased some goods FOB Seller's Plant. When the goods arrived at our dock, it was clear they were damaged, so we refused the goods. The carrier took the goods back to the seller, who refused to accept them.

Now the carrier is demanding that we pay them, but the carrier is probably at fault because the carrier signed the BOL without objection at the seller's dock. What do we do? I don't want to pay for the goods because they are non-conforming, but both the carrier and the seller are pointing the finger at each other.

A:

1. As a general rule, if the terms of sale were "FOB Seller's Plant", the risk of loss in transit is on the buyer/consignee. In other words, if conforming goods were tendered by the seller/shipper in good order and condition to the carrier at origin, you will have to pay the seller for the goods, even though they arrived damaged.

2. If there was transit damage (caused by the carrier) you, as the buyer/consignee, should have filed a loss and damage claim with the carrier. Freight charges, if paid, are includable as part of your claim.

3. The claimant (in this case the buyer/consignee) has a duty to "mitigate loss". Unless the goods were damaged so as to be substantially worthless, you probably should have accepted them and attempted some kind of repair or salvage. Since you refused them to the carrier, the carrier also has a duty to mitigate the loss if it is reasonably possible to do so. Any salvage proceeds should be credited against your account.

Salvage - Food Products Damaged in Transit

Q:

Our company ships edible foods, and when product is rejected by a customer, the carriers usually claim that the product is saleable. We usually find, however, that the product is far below our product standards and is not edible. What can we do to protect our company against product liability suits, and recover for the value of goods damaged in transit?

A:

The owner of damaged goods has a right to determine whether or not a shipment meets its quality standards, or is fit for human consumption under F&DA rules. An affidavit from a qualified expert will suffice. If not fit for human consumption, it may have some value for animal feed, and that value must be established and credited to the carrier. The owner must control the disposition of all damaged goods to protect against release of questionable products to the public, at the risk of being sued for personal injury or death from the damaged goods

Salvage - Inspection of Damaged Shrubs

Q:

We had a shipment of shrubs (junipers, etc.) in one gallon containers on the floor of the trailer.

The driver did not run the reefer unit and the shrubs were refused due to heat damage. Now the carrier wants us to inspect all 6000 pieces and determine which ones can possibly be saved. Part of the problem is that you can't really tell whether they will survive without watering them and waiting a few weeks to see what happens. What should we do?

A:

The claimant does have a duty to mitigate damages - sort, segregate & salvage. You should have a USDA or Plant expert inspect the damaged goods and get a formal written report. You can do a representative sample rather than a 100% inspection.

You should file a claim for the entire amount. The amount of the claim can be reduced later if there is salvage value.

Salvage Allowance - Safety Risk

Q:

Our company ships automotive lamps and other types of light bulbs. When a box is damaged the product is no longer safe to use due to the nature of automotive lamps (they may appear useable, however, the testing to determine if they are safe costs more than the bulbs are worth). The carrier maintains that these broken light bulbs have salvage value, but we do not wish to release these bulbs over to the carrier due to the fact a bulb may have internal damage making it a possible fire or explosion hazard. With a product of this nature what type of salvage value would it have?

A:

This is always a gray area, because shippers have an obligation to mitigate damages when it is reasonable, under the circumstances, to do so.

You make two good arguments for not allowing salvage: (1) the cost of testing exceeds the value of the light bulbs, and (2) there is a legitimate concern over exposure for product liability.

I would think that if you make these points known to the carrier, it should pay the claim in full and not expect a salvage allowance.

Salvage Allowance; Arbitrary Percentage

Q:

We ship resin, which can become contaminated in transit. Once a package is opened, the resin can become contaminated by dirt, pieces of packaging or other foreign material that can jam processing machinery or cause flaws in the finished products. Moisture can also cause problems for our customers, and therefore, they absolutely refuse to accept any product when the package has been compromised. Therefore, our corporate quality control policy requires that all damaged product be returned by carriers, and we deduct a 10% salvage allowance on our claims. Some carriers claim that they can sell this damaged product for 25%. How do we proceed to resolve this dispute?

A:

Your policy of requiring the return of all damaged product is the correct procedure when contaminated product can cause further damage or injury. However, the problem is that any arbitrary percentage for a salvage allowance is just that: arbitrary. Obviously, the shipper wants the product to be returned to prevent it entering the market as distressed merchandise, and possibly compromising its trade name, reputation for quality, etc. or creating a possible product liability or warranty problem. If the product is not substantially worthless due to the damage, the shipper does have a duty to mitigate damages and attempt to salvage what it can. (See Freight Claims in Plain English (3rd Ed. 1995) at Section 10.9 - 10.10 for a detailed discussion.) However, 10% (or 25%) may not reflect the real salvage value. You really should attempt to determine what it actually costs to inspect, handle, re-process, re-package, etc. and what the salvaged product can be sold for. Then you will be in a better position to argue with the carrier as to the proper amount as a salvage allowance.

P.S. If the shipper has a written transportation contract with its carriers, it can include provisions governing salvage of damaged product and avoid this kind of dispute.

Salvage Value - Returned Damaged Freight

Q:

When our freight is delivered in damaged condition we have the carrier return the freight to us to protect our product name. Although the carrier agrees to return the freight, it denies our claim for damages because it has agreed to return the damaged freight to us. Can they do this?

A:

No. The carrier is entitled to a credit for the salvage value, if any, to reduce the amount of the damage claim and may even charge you freight charges for the return shipment. (Since you want the freight returned to you, it would be incumbent upon you to establish the salvage value.) But the carrier cannot simply decline the claim because it agreed to return the damaged freight.

Shipper Liability for "Dropped Trailers"

Q:

Our carrier drops reefer trailers at our facility which we subsequently load. What sort of liability are we incurring, if any?

A:

There are really two issues involved with regard to carrier trailers dropped at your facility for loading. First, you may become a "bailee" of the equipment, i.e., since you have possession and control over another person's property, you become responsible for it. You could become liable if the trailer is damaged (or stolen) while on your premises. Your should have your risk manager or insurance department check to make sure your general liability policy adequately covers the equipment.

Second, you should always inspect trailers before loading product into them, especially refrigerated food products. Any trailer that is defective, dirty, etc. should be rejected. There should be no additional liability exposure because you inspected a carrier's equipment.

You should note that there is a line of cases involving liability for improper loading, where the improper loading causes an accident (load shift, cargo falling off the truck, etc.) or an injury to a driver, shipping/receiving employee, etc.

Liability, as between the shipper and carrier, usually turns on whether the defect is "latent" or "patent". However, as far as the carrier's equipment is concerned, it is clear that federal (FHWA) regulations make the carrier primarily liable for the safety of its equipment.

Shipper's Duty - Proper Loading

Q:

I heard about a court decision which said that a shipper has a common law duty to verify its carrier has properly secured its load for shipment. This bothers me tremendously, I do not see how a company can be held responsible for an area that is not within a company's expertise.

The securing of loads should be left up to the carriers who are both responsible and have the experience in this area, not people out on a company's floor.

A:

According to a number of recent court decisions, shippers do have a common law duty to properly prepare, package, etc. and, if the shipper does the loading, to do it safely. On the other hand, both the case law and the federal DOT/FHWA regulations make it clear that the carrier is responsible to check the load and make sure it is properly secured.

Shipper's Load & Count - Multiple Stop-off Shipments

Q:

Our carrier has denied a shortage claim on the basis that the shipment was "Shippers Load & Count." In addition, the shipment involves multiple stop-offs. What should we do?

A:

If the shipment was actually "SL&C", the burden of proof essentially shifts to the shipper as to what was loaded into the trailer. In other words, if there is a shortage at delivery, the shipper must establish, through appropriate testimony, documents, etc. that the goods were actually tendered to the carrier at the origin.

If you load, count and seal the trailer and the driver is not present to witness the loading, it is properly a SL&C shipment. Merely asking a driver to break the seal (at origin) and look into a trailer loaded to full visible capacity would probably not change the nature of the SL&C shipment as there is no way for the driver to verify the pallet or carton count.

On multiple stop-off shipments, the driver is responsible to make sure that the right pallets or cartons are delivered to the right consignee, and get a count and signature on the delivery receipt. Your best protection is to require your carriers to provide copies of delivery receipts as a condition for payment of their freight bills.

Shipping Records - Retention

Q:

In light of latest provisions of the ICC Termination what period of time do you recommend for retention of shipping documents? I would like to prepare a uniform document retention plan for our Distribution Centers.

A:

We generally recommend a minimum of 3 1/2 years to retain freight bills and bills of lading. The reasoning is that the statute of limitations on recovery of freight charges by a carrier is now 18 months and statutes of limitation can be extended by 2 years if a carrier files for bankruptcy.

Shortages - Rail Shipments

Q:

Is the railroad liable for shortages when a car is shipped from a warehouse without a signed bill of lading, and delivered without a consignee's signature?

A:

As a general rule, the railroad is still a "common carrier" and should be liable for loss or damage occurring in its possession. However, your rail boxcar shipments are probably exempt and subject to the railroad's "exempt circular" (tariff). Most rail circulars provide that the railroad will not accept liability without physical evidence of a forced entry into the car. Railroads usually will not pay shortage claims if there is a sealed car and the seals are intact at the destination.

Rail cars should be sealed immediately upon loading, their seals checked before opening the doors, and product counted carefully during unloading. Doors and seals must be carefully checked and their condition recorded before removing product from the rail site. Shortages should be reported immediately to allow the carrier to inspect the car, its doors, seals, etc. Keep the seals and show them to the rail inspector if you suspect tampering.

Special Damages - Customer Chargebacks

Q:

I have two concerns about special damages.

First, we have a customer that has been charging us approximately $100-$200 per shipment if the envelope of related documents (packing list) is missing. We list this envelope on the bill of lading as a piece of freight, and the driver signs for all the freight, including the envelope of related documents.

When I filed a claim against the carrier for the missing envelope, the carrier denied the claim, because it doesn't represent "full actual loss, damage, or injury to such property.

"They also attached a portion Miller's Law, Fourth Edition to emphasize their point. In other words, the carrier believes that our company or our customer is trying to make a profit from this claim.

On the other hand, aren't we alerting the carrier to the value of the envelope by listing it on the bill of lading? Shouldn't the carrier be liable, since they signed for the envelope, and they lost it? What is a reasonable charge for a missing envelope of related documents?

Second, we have several customers that are charging us approximately $100 per shipment for bad pallets. I filed a claim for $100.00 for bad pallets. We tendered the freight to the carrier on slip sheets, and the carrier placed the freight on pallets for their own convenience. When the shipment delivered, the customer documented "5 bad pallets" on the delivery receipt. Despite this, the carrier is denying my claim, because it falls under special damages. Shouldn't the carrier be liable for providing unsolicited pallets to our customer?

I appreciate any help, as more customers are starting to charge us for errors of this nature.

A:

1. The carrier is definitely liable for the loss of your document package. However, the question is: what is the proper measure of damages?

Since you don't "sell" the documents to your customer, or place a dollar value on them in your invoice to the customer, it could be argued that the value is merely the cost to reproduce another set and send it to the customer. The carrier is somewhat correct in arguing that the $100 - $200 "charge" from your customer is "special damages" because it is not within the contemplation of the parties or foreseeable at the time of shipment.

If you want the carrier to be liable for a specific dollar amount, you probably would have to put some explicit language on the bill of lading to the effect that the carrier will be liable for $xxx if the document package is not delivered to the consignee along with the shipment.

Obviously, if you have a transportation agreement with your carrier, this would be a provision which could be negotiated and included in your contract. (We recommend to all our shipper clients that they enter into written transportation contracts with their carriers. If you need assistance in this regard, please contact us.)

There is another issue here also: what gives your customer the right to charge you for missing documents? Is this some provision in the contract of sale or in the purchase order? If not, you don't have to accept the charge.

2. I don't understand how (or why) a customer would charge you for "bad pallets" (or "good pallets" for that matter).

The customer is not paying you for the pallets, and I presume that the pallets would normally be returned to the carrier. You shouldn't be involved in this at all, and the same comment as above (is there a provision in the contract of sale or purchase order) applies here also.

Special Damages - Express Freight Charges

Q:

We ship transformers that are manufactured in Puerto Rico and then warehoused in El Paso, TX. When a transformer is damaged it often has to be sent back to Puerto Rico for the repairs to be made. However, because the customer often needs to have the product back quickly, it needs to be sent back by air. Is the LTL carrier responsible for damaging the transformer obligated to pay this additional expense, and if not, what can we recover?

A:

Questions as to recoverable damages require analysis of the specific facts and circumstances of each shipment. There are cases in which express freight charges for replacement of lost or damaged shipments have been allowed, and cases in which they have been denied (as "special damages").

In this situation, it could be argued that the air freight charges are reasonable and foreseeable as an effort to mitigate the damage, i.e., to have the transformer repaired and delivered to the consignee as promptly as possible.

Be prepared, however, for the carrier to say that the air freight charges are "special damages" because it was not given notice of the consequences of failure to deliver with reasonable dispatch.

Statutes and Regulations

Q:

Can you tell me what are the important DOT, OSHA, or any other regulations or laws that may apply to the transportation industry? Particularly to shipping docks and land transportation.

A:

The principal statute is the Interstate Commerce Act (Title 49 of the U.S. Code), and the principal regulations are the DOT and Federal Highway Administration regulations. I should also mention that The Transportation Consumer Protection Council publishes a monthly Trans Digest which covers a variety of current issues including cargo security, loss and damage, etc.

There are also texts and other educational materials dealing with loss and damage, although not specifically with the role of a security manager.

Storage on Refused Shipments

Q:

This question applies primarily to LTL transportation. When can a carrier begin charging storage on refused shipments? I have been unable to find anything in the NMFC rules that sets time limits on this.

Depending on the carrier and the business volume associated with a specific carrier, the rules seem to change. Since I handle multiple shipping locations, I am trying to get some consistency in our OS&D program and would like to know if there are any rules governing storage and the carrier's obligation to notify the shipper (as well as the required mode of notification) on refused shipments.

A:

Assuming that you are shipping by common carrier under a Uniform Straight Bill of Lading, the relevant provisions are found in Section 4 of the terms and conditions on the reverse side of the bill of lading. This section provides

"If the consignee refuses the shipment... the carrier's liability shall then become that of a warehouseman. Carrier shall promptly attempt to provide notice...to the shipper of party, if any, designated to receive notice on this bill of lading.... Storage charges, based on the carrier's tariff, shall start no sooner than the next business day following the attempted notification..."

In other words, the Uniform Straight Bill of Lading essentially defers to the individual carrier's tariff for details as to storage rates and rules.

This is one of the reasons why shippers must always be careful to demand a copy of the carrier's rules tariff before doing business, since these tariffs contain the rules governing storage charges (as well as other rules governing accessorial charges, credit terms, liability limitations, etc.).

I would point out that the problems you discuss can be obviated by a properly drafted Transportation Contract, and we always recommend that our clients use such contracts with their motor carriers.

Surface Transportation Board

Q:

What is the Surface Transportation Board? What responsibilities and/or authority does it have in relation to freight transportation?

A:

The Surface Transportation Board was created by the ICC Termination Act of 1995 (effective 1/1/96) to take over the remaining responsibilities of the ICC after it was "sunset" by Congress. The STB has some of the powers of the former ICC to investigate complaints, adjudicate disputes, and to enforce specified provisions of the Interstate Commerce Act, such as the freight undercharge provisions in the Negotiated Rates Act.

Other regulatory functions of the former ICC were transferred to the Federal Highway Administration or to the Secretary of Transportation.

Tariffs - Participation by Carriers

Q:

s a carrier required to execute a power of attorney to participate in a collectively-made
ariff that has been obtained by a shipper through a license agreement for the purpose of
stablishing rates in a contract between the carrier and shipper?

:

Carriers are required to "participate" through a power of attorney all in collectively-
nade tariffs, e.g., the National Motor Freight Classification or the class rate tariffs
ublished by the rate bureaus.

Iowever, you have to distinguish between collectively-made tariffs and proprietary
ariff products which they may publish. For example, Czar-Lite is a proprietary product
f SMC. As such, carriers would not have to participate if you want to incorporate Czar-
Lite into your transportation agreement.

ime Limits - Collecting Freight Charges

):

represent a motor carrier and filed an action for unpaid freight charges and penalties
n state court. Prior to suit the shipper was represented by a freight consultant who
lisputed the classification of the freight and therefore the rate charged. Although most
f the invoices were more than eighteen months old at the time, he never mentioned a
tatute of limitations defense. When I filed the lawsuit, one of the twelve invoices was
vithin the eighteen month statute of limitation period.

he shipper's attorney raised a statute of limitations defense to all but the one invoice.

)oes the statute of limitations run from the date of last account activity, e.g., charge or
)ayment, or is each invoice viewed separately? Does the fact that part of the amount
)eing sued for is penalties and not freight charges per se make a difference as to the
unning of the statute? Is there any way to keep the case in state court where the state
tatute of limitations (3 years) would apply?

)oes a partial payment on an invoice change the time from which the statute is deemed
o begin running?

\:

   "A carrier providing transportation or service subject to civil action to recover charges
or transportation or service provided by the carrier within 18 months after the claim
rises."

As a general rule, this statute of limitations is applicable to any interstate transportation of property by motor carrier with the exception of (1) property which is "exempt" and (2) property transported under a written transportation contract pursuant to where the contract expressly waives the provisions of the statute.

Time Limits - International Air Freight; Partial Loss

Q:

Last fall we uncovered a clever scheme by someone wherein they were resealing opened cartons with a tape that camouflaged their activity/theft. Unfortunately, several cartons from previous shipments were not uncovered until ten days after receipt. In our operation, we have a "case reserve" situation where only cartons/items that are required in our "active picking" warehouse are opened and checked in (or if there is evidence of pilferage).

I reported these concealed/post-dated freight claims to our forwarding agent who prepared a "notice of concealed pilferage" to airlines. I subsequently filed a freight claim with the air carrier. Our insurance company in Italy last week informed me that due to the passing of "7 days after receipt" on filing "notice of concealed pilferage," they will not honor claim. Claim is for around $3000.

A:

I assume this is an international shipment, in which case the air carrier's liability is governed by the Warsaw Convention. Article 26 of the Convention states that "...in the case of damage" a claim must be made within 7 days from the date of receipt of the goods.

However, this section does not specifically address a non-delivery or partial loss. The court decisions come up with different (and sometimes conflicting) results, depending on the particular facts and the terms and conditions of the air waybill. You may well be able to avoid the 7-day time limit, based on what you have outlined.

Time Limits for Filing Overcharges

Q:

We used a transport tanker company for over two years and shipped to several customers on a regular basis. We do not have a signed contract. Our problem is that the freight charges have not been consistent, even on similar shipments. How far back can we go to seek relief from the transport company for overcharged invoices?

A:

The first question is what was the basis of the original rates? Were these negotiated over the phone, documented in writing in any way, based on the carrier's tariffs, or what? In order to have an "overcharge" you must have some agreement as to what rate was supposed to be charged. It is difficult to answer your question without this information.

The answer would also depend on whether the transportation involved was interstate or intrastate. If the shipments were intrastate, it is possible the state's statute of limitations for contracts may govern (which varies from state to state, but generally ranges from 3 to 6 years).

"If a shipper seeks to contest the charges originally billed or additional charges subsequently billed, the shipper may request that the [Surface Transportation] Board determine whether the charges billed must be paid.

A shipper must contest the original bill or subsequent bill within 180 days of receipt of the bill in order to have the right to contest such charges."

Most motor carriers interpret this section to mean that overcharge claims must be submitted within 180 days or they will be time-barred.

Furthermore, even if you "contest" the freight bills within 180 days, requires that a civil action must be commenced within 18 months after the claim accrues.

Time Limits: Exceptions to "9-Month" Rule for Filing Claims

Q:

Are there any exceptions to the rule that a claim must be filed within 9 months or the carrier need not pay it? We filed a claim form but left the "Amount of Claim" box blank because we didn't know the exact amount of our loss. The carrier's agent told us that we should file the claim immediately even if we didn't know the amount actually lost.

A:

Yes, there are exceptions. However, the first question should be whether the documentation filed within 9 months met the legal requirements for a claim. The regulations require that the claim state a "specified or determinable amount of money." Therefore, some amount must be stated, preferable the maximum value of the shipment, or an estimate of that value. If no amount is stated, some courts have found under these circumstances that no claim was filed within the 9 months limit.

When an estimated amount was stated within 9 months, the 9th Circuit has held that a claim was sufficient even when the actual loss was not determined until later.

As to your being told by the carrier's agent that it wasn't necessary to know the amount of loss before filing, some courts have applied the principles of waiver and estoppel under similar circumstances.

Time Limits; 9-Month Limit for Filing Claims

Q:

Is there any way to get around the fact that a claim was not filed against a carrier within 9 months? The carrier was notified by telephone of a $12 million claim in time, and we attempted to salvage the damaged goods, but failed to finalize the claim until after 9 months.

A:

Assuming that the shipment moved on a uniform straight bill of lading, the shipper was required to file a claim in writing within 9 months of the date of delivery. The court decisions generally uphold the 9-month time limit in the uniform bill of lading, with only a few exceptions. I would say that, even though there were other communications that might have led the shipper to believe the carrier was still considering its claim, this would still not cure the late filing. However, a claim of this size would appear to warrant extensive research and study of the facts and circumstances.

Transportation Contracts - Requirements

Q:

Is there any need to include "distinct needs" or refer to a "series of shipments" in new motor carrier contracts? I know I should purchase your model contracts disk, but I am wrestling with a deadline. My feeling is that motor contracts no longer require these little tricks.

A:

Technically, there is no longer a requirement for "distinct needs" or "a series of shipments" in a motor carrier contract. The previous ICC regulations were eliminated and the statutory requirements were superseded by the ICC Termination Act of 1995. The only statutory provision (49 USC 14101) says that a carrier "may enter into a contract with a shipper... to provide specified services under specified rates and conditions..."

We still include language in the boiler plate contract which refers to distinct needs and a series of shipments (out of an abundance of caution); this is only because if a contract were to be questioned, it might be easier to convince a court that the transportation services were contract as opposed to common carriage.

Truck Drivers - Overtime

Q:

I have searched but have never been able to find any of the laws that actually exclude the trucking industry from paying their employees "overtime" when working in excess of the "standard" 40 hour week.

I fully understand the regulations concerning the 70 hour/8 day rules and 60 hour/7 day laws, BUT those are plainly stated as MAXIMUMS.

In the State I live in (Utah) there are numerous trucking companies who never pay their drivers ANY overtime, regardless of how many hours they work.

I guess I have a couple of questions for now: 98

1. Can a Company "force" you to work more than 40 hours in any consecutive 7 day period?

2. If you do work the full 70 hours in 8 days, why no overtime after 40 hours?

It appears to me that this has just become more of a "standard practice" instead of being actual laws.

A:

The answer to your question involves the interaction of a number of federal and state laws. I would suggest the following:

1. If you are a member of a union, contact your union representative. Overtime compensation is usually covered in the collective bargaining agreement between the union and the employer.

2. If you are not in a union, contact the personnel or human resources department in your company and ask them about the company's overtime policy.

3. If you are not satisfied with the result, contact the local office of the department of labor in your state.

Unreasonable Rules in Railroad Contracts

Q:

I need your opinion on the following matter. Railroads often insert statements like "we must be notified of damage or shortage within 24hrs of delivery". This statement seems somewhat unreasonable in real terms. They then use this statement to decline claims not reported within the specified period.

Is this valid? Shouldn't there also be a statement that says they will decline claims for damage not reported within their terms?

Is this a legal procedure?

Any light you can shed on this would be greatly appreciated.

A:

Check your railroad contracts or Exempt Circulars for the claim rules. Some require 24 hr. notice as a condition for liability. Yes, this is unreasonable, and should be negotiated out of the agreement at its inception. There are many other unreasonable rules in railroad contracts.

What's in a Name? - Carrier Mergers and Shipper Liability

Q:

We are experiencing carrier mergers, acquisitions, etc., and are receiving bills of lading with the old carrier's name on them.

Are we safe in continuing to ship on these bills without naming the new carrier? Some say "an affiliate of _____".

A:

Based on our experiences with undercharge cases, shippers must insist on legally correct bills of lading and contracts showing the proper carrier name. Bankruptcy lawyers will attempt to renounce any contract in the name of a carrier that was merged or acquired unless there has been an adoption of the contract or tariff. A properly drawn contract would have a clause referring to the assumption of the contract by successors, but only with the shipper's consent. Without such a restriction, a shipper could readily acquire a contract carrier controlled by undesirable interests.

Freight Broker Industry Statistics and Facts

Nearly all goods transported in the United States move by truck at some point in the journey. Trucks carry over 60% of the annual gross tonnage moved in the US, making trucking the "backbone" of the intermodal (AIR, SEA, LAND) transportation network.

Each day millions of big rig tractor trailers (also known as semi-trucks, 18-wheelers and motor carriers) move freight throughout the United States from one destination to another. These rigs pull various types of cargo ranging from perishable foods, consumer goods to general cargo. In fact, 70% of all manufactured and retail goods transported within the US on an annual basis are via truck.

Transportation occurs daily, over $12,000,000,000,000 (trillion) dollars per year globally. Transportation within the US exceeds $1 trillion annually, of which US trucking represents well over $300 billion.

FACT: Nearly all goods transported in the United States move by truck at some point in the journey. Trucks carry over 60% of the annual gross tonnage moved in the U.S., making trucking the "backbone" of the intermodal (AIR, SEA, LAND) transportation network. Freight Broker Career refers to this extraordinary FACT as the "Truck Supply Chain."

The following concepts are provided for the benefit of non-industry professionals to help create a shared understanding of the transportation marketplace.

Each day millions of big rig tractor trailers (also known as semi-trucks, 18-wheelers and motor carriers) move freight throughout the United States from one destination to another. These rigs pull various types of cargo ranging from perishable foods, consumer goods to general cargo. In fact, 70% of all manufactured and retail goods transported within the U.S. on an annual basis are via truck. To put things into perspective, the U.S. transportation marketplace generates over one trillion dollars in revenues annually, of which U.S. trucking represents well over $300 billion. U.S. Freight Brokers offers the concept of "U.S. Strategic Trucks" and "U.S. Strategic Freight" to help the reader comprehend the complexity and enormous scale of this industry.

The Motor Carrier's Challenge

A typical long-haul outbound load covers a distance of 1,000 miles. For motor carriers, the outbound haul is where they can selectively evaluate a load's profitability prior to accepting a contract to move it. However the return haul, known as a back-haul, is harder for the carrier to estimate in advance since in most cases the back-haul is not known until the carrier is near its current load's destination. It is not uncommon for long-haul truckers to have to wait in a location for a few days for a suitable and profitable back-haul load that allows them to return at or near their operating base.

The alternative to waiting is to "dead-head," a trucking term describing when a truck travels without a load, sometimes up to several hundred miles, to meet a new load or to travel back to base empty. Therefore, coordinating a well paying back-haul load within a suitable geographic area allows strategic truckers to maximize profitability since trucks that are not hauling freight are still subject to fixed overhead costs (e.g., insurance, medical, licensing fees, etc.). The objective of the strategic trucker is to maximize loads carried while reducing dead-head miles. Hence the motor carrier's challenge of finding a suitable back-haul load immediately is critical to maximizing profitability, and more importantly, getting back home to family and friends as soon as possible.

The Shipper's Challenge

To help explain the shipper's challenge the reader must understand that trucking capacity, unlike the airline industry, is very difficult to forecast accurately beyond seven days. Complicating the issue is that shippers' delivery schedules are not consistent and frequently change based on the needs and consumption patterns of its end-users. To illustrate, think of your favorite retailer and a popular product it carries. Your retailer will order replacement inventory as needed, and depending on the season, this could be daily, weekly, or quarterly. Once an order is placed, the retailer calls the manufacturer (i.e., the shipper) to provide more inventory. To fill this order, the shipper must locate available transportation to get the freight to the retailer just in time for the big ale. Witness the birth of a market where hundreds of thousands of different retailers all place shipping orders each day in a dynamic and sometimes chaotic marketplace.

The shipper's challenge is to quickly identify, quality, reliable and available transportation in an ever increasing fragmented marketplace.

Growth through globalization

Throughout history the oceans have been important to people around the world as a means of transportation. Unlike a few decades ago, however, ships are now carrying goods rather than people. Since the rise of intercontinental air travel, sea travel has become limited to shorter trips (ferry services across the Baltic and North Seas, the Mediterranean, Japan and Southeast Asia) and recreational cruises. The latter have recently experienced a tremendous boom and represent an increasingly lucrative source of tourist income.

As markets became increasingly globalized, shipping volumes soared. From the 1950s to the latest global economic crisis, the growth rate of international trade was almost consistently twice that of economic activity as a whole. From 2000 to 2008 world trade increased by an average 5.4 per cent each year, while economic activity, as measured by the global Gross Domestic Product (GDP), increased by only 3 per cent per annum.

Due to the spectacular rise of trade vis-à-vis economic growth, world trade since the 1950s has more than trebled to 45 per cent of the global GDP, while goods destined for the processing industry have in fact more than quadrupled.

With respect to the value of the goods, about 23 per cent of world trade is between countries with a common border. This percentage has remained fairly constant over recent decades. Between continents, however, it differs a great deal depending on their level of development. In Europe and North America the proportion is the highest at 25 to 35 per cent. This trade is predominantly transacted by road and rail. Cargo between countries without a common border is carried mainly by sea, although increasing quantities of manufactured goods are being forwarded by air. Growth rates for air freight are more than double those for shipping in recent years. Which mode of transport handles how much cargo depends on the (relative) transportation costs and the value-to-weight ratio of the goods – the higher the value per unit of weight, the less significant the cost of transportation. Punctuality and reliability are considered more important for valuable commodities.

According to research by economists, higher-income households purchase higher-quality products.

The residents of wealthy countries therefore tend to buy more quality goods. Accordingly, rising incomes influence the demand for transport in three ways. First, quality goods are more expensive. Their value-to-weight ratio is therefore higher and the cost of transporting them is lower compared to their value. Second, as incomes rise, consumers are more likely to purchase certain expensive products and fancy goods. At the same time they expect to receive the articles within a very short time. Third, the delivery period itself is a key element of product quality, having an increasing influence on purchasing decisions; customers are no longer prepared to tolerate long delays. All of these factors have contributed to the even higher growth rates of air freight in comparison to shipping.

What fuels maritime traffic

As mentioned, the main reason behind the massive increase in shipping was the growth in world trade. But institutional and technological factors also had a role to play. In the past, the liberalization achievements of GATT and its successor the WTO provided a new momentum to world trade. China's economic opening to the outside world, which led to their admission to the WTO in 2001, was also very significant – its exports quadrupled within 5 years. Another example of integrated markets boosting international trade is a trebling of exports from Mexico to the USA within 6 years of NAFTA being established.

The appetites of the industrial nations and newly-industrializing emerging economies, particularly China and India, for energy and mineral resources led to increasing quantities of goods being transported from far-distant countries.

The information and communications technology revolution dramatically reduced the costs of mobility and accessibility. It allowed new network connections and production processes such as just-in-time production, outsourcing and offshoring, and provided a tremendous stimulus to logistics.

As a result of rising demand, transportation costs fell. Ships increased in size. Economies of scale were exploited. Furthermore, there were technological advances and organizational improvements in port management – of general cargo traffic, for instance. Of overriding importance was containerization, the greatest transportation revolution of the 20th century.

Industry Snapshot

Companies primarily engaged in operating vessels for the transportation of freight on the deep seas between the United States and foreign ports. Establishments operating vessels for the transportation of freight that travel to foreign ports and also to noncontiguous territories are included in this industry.

Deep sea foreign transportation of freight is greatly influenced by the global economy and international competition. U.S. companies in this industry compete with each other and with foreign carriers. U.S. regulations have tended to make costs higher for U.S. ship owners than for those ships bearing the flags of other nations. To stay competitive in the cargo transport business, many U.S.-owned ships carry flags of nations with lower expenses. By operating under the authority of other countries, labor costs for U.S. shipping operations could be cut as much as 80 percent.

Although tonnage of foreign merchandise trade increased in the early twenty-first century, rising costs and price competition continued to mean declining profits for U.S. ship owners. Some shipping firms received subsidies from the U.S. government to compensate for high U.S. flag operating costs. These subsidies fell under the Maritime Security Program that would make steamships available to the U.S. Defense Department should the need arise. According to the U.S. Census Bureau, total revenues in the deep sea freight transportation industry reached $9.6 billion in 2009, and the U.S. Transportation Institute estimated that by the early 2010s, 1.3 billion metric tons of cargo were being moved by ship annually.

The outlook for the U.S. flag fleet was predicated on several factors, including foreign competitors; costs of labor, fuel, insurance, and other operating expenses; and volume of trade in relation to available cargo space. Overcapacity has been a problem for U.S. and foreign merchant fleets for many years, resulting in lower freight rates.

However, an ever-increasing globalization of the marketplace led to growing demand for freight-bearing vessels during the first decade of the 2000s and early 2010s, especially for transporting exports from Asia to the United States.

Organization and Structure

The U.S. merchant deep sea fleet is made up of three categories of service: liner, non-liner (or tramp), and tanker.

Liner service includes regular, scheduled stops at ports along a route. Vessels operating as liners may be owned or chartered by an operator. Operators must accept any legal cargo they are equipped to carry, unless it does not meet the minimum freight requirements of the operator. Liner service usually carries manufactured goods.

Often, two or more carriers along a route form "conferences" in order to regulate rates and competition. All conference members must charge the same freight rates, although rates may fluctuate according to supply and demand for cargo space. Liner service vessels are designed to handle the cargo most often shipped along their routes. Trip frequency depends upon the demands for shipping along that route.

Non-liner, or tramp, shipping is scheduled individually by a customer who charters the ship to carry its cargo. Tramps usually carry only one type of bulk cargo, such as coal, ores, grain, lumber, or sugar. On occasion, two shippers of the same commodity may charter the ship jointly. Freight rates vary depending on the negotiations of the ship owner and shipper and the supply of and demand for cargo space. The tramp freight market peaked in 1995 and continued to decline except for a few peak rate periods.

Tankers carry liquid cargoes, especially crude oil and petroleum products. Tankers may be operated by privately owned companies for charter or by the oil company or other company as part of its entire industrial organization. Oil companies also charter extra ships as needed. However, they are not the only ones to employ ships exclusively for their own trade. Other companies may have specialized ships for transport of their goods. For instance, produce growing and distributing concerns operate fleets of refrigerated vessels for transportation purposes.

Some companies chartered ships on a long-term basis. Doing so provided many of the same advantages of owning a fleet without the enormous investment. By owning a fleet or contracting for long-term charter, the shipper was able to maintain complete control over shipping schedules. It could divert its ships to ports where demand for the product was high, and it could engage for service a fleet of ships with crews that had experience in handling a particular commodity.

Ships became increasingly more specialized during the twentieth century, and specialized ships were built to carry such diverse products as bulk cement, liquid chemicals, coal, iron ore, liquefied natural gas, newsprint and other paper products, petroleum and petroleum products, wood chips and wood pulp, refrigerated foods, and heavy equipment like railroad locomotives or electric generator parts. Because many specialized ships were expensive to build, a ship owner could agree to have a ship built for a company with the stipulation that the company agree to lease the ship for most of its active life.

There were several federal agencies that administered laws and policies concerning the U.S. merchant fleet. The main agency was the U.S. Department of Transportation Maritime Administration (MARAD), which was charged with coordinating the requirements of ship owners, shipbuilders, shippers, and labor unions for both domestic and foreign trade. In the late twentieth century, MARAD initiated and administered construction and operating subsidies, capital construction funds, and market development and maritime training.

Background and Development

Since the earliest days of the business in the United States, the federal government has considered the maintenance of a viable merchant fleet to be a priority for national security and the health of foreign trade. During wars and other emergencies, the U.S. military chartered private ships to transport supplies.

Congressional legislation throughout U.S. history has helped to protect and promote the U.S. merchant fleet. Legislation in 1845 required the U.S. Postal Service to transport mail abroad on U.S. merchant ships. Mail contracts were offered as incentives for shipping companies to establish shipping lines with Cuba, Panama, and major European ports. The law also stipulated that merchant ships could be converted to warships if necessary. The Military Transportation Act, passed in 1904, directed the U.S. Army and Navy to give preference to U.S. flagships for the transportation of supplies for direct support of military operations abroad.

The Merchant Marine Act of 1928 offered incentives to the shipbuilding industry to build new ships so U.S. fleets could compete more effectively in the world market. This legislation, however, failed to spur the construction of many new ships, and U.S. foreign shipping continued to decline as it had for many years.

The Merchant Marine Act of 1936 has been called the Magna Carta for U.S. shipping. It called for the first direct aid to merchant fleets for construction and operation. It also authorized the government to build ships and charter them to private companies for operation on foreign routes if private citizens did not provide that service. It required subsidized fleets to set up special funds to replace aging ships, provided loans and mortgage insurance, and authorized a training program for U.S. crew members.

The landmark legislation was followed in 1954 by the "Fifty-Fifty Law," which required that at least half of the country's foreign aid or humanitarian aid cargoes be carried abroad by U.S. merchant ships.

A weak merchant marine was regarded as unacceptable to the U.S. Department of Defense, as the military has historically relied on private ships to carry military cargo during emergencies. Although all U.S. presidents since George Washington have recognized the importance of a strong merchant marine for the nation's security, the industry has not always received the support it needed to remain viable and to compete successfully with foreign ship operators. Presidents George H.W. Bush and Bill Clinton promised reform in order to maintain the shrinking U.S. merchant fleet, which carried only about 15 percent of U.S. exports in the early 1990s, according to The Wall Street Journal. The National Performance Review headed by former Vice President Al Gore made several reform recommendations regarding the maritime industry, including striking down legislation that forced U.S. flag ships to carry military and aid cargoes, curtailing subsidies, repealing antitrust protection for carrier conferences established under the 1984 Shipping Act, and extending the U.S. flag to carrier lines that had foreign investors.

The Merchant Marine Act of 1970 was an attempt to counter several growing problems in the shipping industry. The U.S. fleet at that time carried only a small portion of the nation's foreign trade, and a large portion of its ships were due to be scrapped because of age within the next few years. The 1970 legislation called for the construction of 300 merchant ships, deferred taxes for U.S. shipping companies if the money was put into funds to replace aging vessels, and provided operating and construction subsidies.

Despite the best intentions and stated policies of the U.S. government, U.S. companies engaged in foreign deep sea transportation have been in trouble for many years. Operation Desert Shield and Operation Desert Storm, the 1990-1991 confrontation with Iraq over its invasion of Kuwait, required a gigantic shipping effort to bring U.S. supplies and equipment to the Middle East. The military enlisted the services of the merchant marine for this task. It also used several dozen chartered transport ships it kept fully loaded and ready. However, even these privately owned ships could not handle the demand of military shipments, and the United States was forced to turn to foreign transport to carry equipment and supplies. During the build-up of forces, almost half of the 200 ships carrying equipment to Saudi Arabia were foreign-owned. This dependence on foreign vessels was partially a consequence of the U.S. fleet's incompatibility with military needs. The U.S. military needed Ro/Ro (roll on/roll off) ships for ease of transport, but Fortune magazine asserted that half the U.S. fleet consisted of oil tankers and the rest were containerships or bulk carriers. Fortune also noted that although ships were much larger than in 1950, the U.S. shipping capacity had decreased a third since then.

Like the rest of the world's fleets, U.S. bulk carriers and supertankers were aged and worn. However, replacing them was expensive, and the perennially shaky financial standing of the industry left it unable to afford replacements. After years of debate, the U.S. Congress finally passed the Maritime Security Act in 1996 by an overwhelming margin. The Act reformed outdated maritime regulations and ensured that privately owned merchant ships would be available to meet national security sealift requirements. It also established a program to provide participating carriers with $1 billion in operating assistance over 10 years.

Prior to passage of the Act, the two largest U.S. shipping companies, American President Companies and CSX Corporation's Sea-Land Service, Inc., considered registering their fleets overseas and flying the flag of another nation unless the United States relaxed its rules and regulations, which ship owners regarded as prohibitively expensive. One of those restrictive rules stated that shipping lines must buy ships built in the United States in order to receive operating subsidies. John Lillie, president of the American President Lines Ltd. (APL), said that ship lines needed to have more freedom to buy vessels overseas because of the lower costs of those products.

Despite threats that even surpassed the passage of the Maritime Security Act, in January 1997, APL chose to remain a U.S. flag carrier, retaining at least a 51 percent U.S. ownership, by enrolling nine of its largest ships in the Maritime Security Program in return for $2.1 million per ship in annual subsidies for $18.9 million. Its other 38 vessels were enrolled in December 1996. Nevertheless, APL Limited announced in April 1997 that it was merging with Neptune Orient Lines LTD, a Singapore-owned and operated steamship line. Sea-Land Services, Inc., also applied to the Maritime Security Program. The U.S. government accepted 15 of its ships in return for $2.1 million per year for each ship participating in the program.

Legislation to deregulate the ocean shipping industry continued to be debated in Congress after the National Industrial Transportation League proposed the issue in January 1995. Such reform would enable shippers to operate in a more certain regulatory environment and, according to steamship lines, would improve shipper-carrier relations and the efficiency of U.S. exporters, as well as reduce the federal government's involvement in unnecessary regulation.

In March 1997, legislation to allow confidential contracting between individual ocean common carriers and shippers, along with measures like publicizing tariffs and the reducing the time required to post tariff rate increases, were proposed to change the Shipping Act of 1984.

Called the Ocean Shipping Reform Act, the bill essentially eliminated the Federal Maritime Commission (FMC) and transferred its functions to an expanded and renamed took effect in 1998 with the FMC eliminated in 1999.

Tankers and Oil Spill Legislation.
Transport of oil in bulk began in the late 1880s. Tankers in the more than 100 years since then have changed dramatically, with ship work handled more by computers, cutting the size of the crew. The enormous size of the tankers of the modern era has also increased the risk of oil spills and the impact such spills have on the environment. The Alaskan oil spill in Prince William Sound by the Exxon Valdez in 1989, which caused significant ecological damage to the area, served as a catalyst in the institution of stricter environmental regulations for tankers and other vessels.

A U.S. law passed in 1990 required all tankers sailing in U.S. waters to be equipped with double hulls to prevent spills if the outer hull was damaged. The shipping industry claimed that another rule included in the act could shut down the shipping industry in U.S. waters. The rule required carriers to provide environmental-liability guarantees in the form of insurance, letters of credit, surety bonds, or Protection and Indemnity (P&I) clubs that insured more than 95 percent of the ships traveling in U.S. waters. However, the liability allowed was open-ended, making it impossible to find guarantors. This rule was not implemented pending resolution of the problem.

Although the number of oceangoing vessels dramatically decreased, fleet productivity, in terms of cargo-carrying capacity, improved 42 percent since 1972. The last operating differential subsidy (ODS) contract expired in 2001. In 1999 three companies still held ODS contracts that covered seven vessels in the bulk trades: Ocean Chemical Carriers, Ocean Chemical Transport, and Liberty Maritime. Under the 1996 Maritime Security Program, which had replaced ODS, 47 U.S. flag vessels remained as participants. Companies that were awarded MSP agreements included American Roll-On Roll-Off Carrier, American Ship Management, Central Gulf Lines, Farrell Lines, First American Bulk Carriers, and Waterman Steamship Lines.

The economic boom of the mid-1990s caused many ship owners to replace their aging vessels with new vessels delivered 18 to 24 months later, just when the market plummeted. The Baltic Freight index dropped and Japanese steel production dropped 13 million tons between 1998 and 1999. Seaborne trade in chemical products dropped 1 percent in 1998, and U.S. petrochemical shipments to the Far East dropped 18 percent.

Although domestic business was booming, the Far East crisis left many owners of new vessels "all dressed up with nowhere to go." Consequently, in 1998 demolition of older vessels increased as owners attempted to avoid continued financial losses. The biggest demolition efforts in 1998 were in the Handy size (20/49,999 deadweight) of vessels that were 20 to 25 years old.

During the early years of the first decade of the 2000s, companies engaged in the deep sea foreign transportation of freight contended with a number of different challenges. While reduced levels of consumer and corporate spending, as well as lower production levels, affected shipment volumes, concerns over security and labor issues also plagued the industry. In the wake of a sluggish economic climate, made worse by the terrorist attacks against the United States on September 11, 2001, conditions were especially bleak for carriers operating routes in the North Atlantic. In 2001 and 2002, these companies struggled with dangerously low shipping rates that were taking a toll on carriers' financial health, leading to significant losses. According to Country Views Wire, the market share of member companies of the Trans-Atlantic Conference Agreement decreased significantly from 1994 to 2000, falling from 70 percent to 46 percent. The Conference membership base also was on the decline, falling from 17 shipping lines in 1997 to 7 in 2001. Making matters worse was the fact that trans-Atlantic routes were stagnant compared to trans-Pacific routes that benefited from high-growth nations in regions like Asia.

Shippers on the West Coast also faced challenges. In the fall of 2002, dockworkers at 29 coastal ports staged a lockout that lasted 10 days after the International Longshore and Warehouse Union failed to come to terms with the Pacific Maritime Association. The lockout created a number of significant problems. Hundreds of ships were stranded, leading to congestion at area seaports. In addition to losses that some industry observers estimated would cost shipping companies anywhere from $400 to $600 million, the lockout had a more severe impact on the U.S. economy that reached billions of dollars.

The terrorist assault on the USS Cole in Aden, Yemen, the terrorist attacks of 2001, and the U.S.-led war against terrorism with Iraq in early 2003 all led to heightened concerns about security within the industry, as well as higher insurance rates for shipping companies. Faced with these threats, Congressional leaders and industry experts were challenged with improving security levels without causing significant shipment delays. While it appeared that at least some standing delays were imminent, the industry sought to improve security by using new technology to ensure the integrity of shipments.

Among technologies being evaluated by the U.S. Department of Defense and the U.S. Department of Transportation were so-called "Eseals," metal bolts embedded with radio transmission devices that sent alert signals to a central communication center to warn of any tampering.

Despite the increased demand for overseas container, bulk, and tanker shipping, the U.S. merchant marine remained a minor player in the global deep sea freight transportation industry. In 1999 CSX sold its Sea-Land global division for $800 million to Denmark's Maersk Sealand, which became the world's largest containership company, further weakening the base of U.S.-owned companies. Tanker numbers dropped during the first half of the first decade of the 2000s, falling below 100 ships for the first time in decades.

Roll-on/roll-off numbers increased slightly into the low 30s, and the number of containerships held relatively steady in the low 80s.

The tanker sector of the industry was affected indirectly but dramatically on April 20, 2010, when BP's Deepwater Horizon rig operating off the coast of Louisiana exploded, killing nine people and setting in motion the worst oil spill in U.S. history. By the time the well was capped almost three months later, on July 15, the rig had dumped approximately 205 million gallons of oil into the ocean, causing an estimated $5 billion in damage to the Gulf waters, the coastline, and the livelihoods of those who relied on it. The federal government responded to the disaster by temporarily banning all off-shore oil drilling, a limitation that was gradually lifted beginning that October. However, tighter regulations were put into place in an attempt to prevent future occurrences.

The End of the First Decade of the 2000s.

In 2006 ports held four of the top seven spots as U.S. foreign trade gateways. Los Angeles was first overall with $170 billion in value of shipments ($26.3 billion export, $143.7 billion import); New York was second overall with $149.3 billion ($33.2 billion export, $116.1 billion import); Long Beach, California, was fifth overall with $134.7 billion ($21.4 billion export, $113.3 billion import), and Houston was seventh overall with $102.8 billion ($41.9 billion export, $60.9 billion import).

The international deep sea freight business was robust in the second half of the first decade of the 2000s as imports to the United States, especially from China, increased, causing significant port congestion. The Port of Los Angeles was so overwhelmed during peak seasons in 2004 that some carriers used the Panama Canal to reach the Gulf Coast or East Coast ports.

In 2007 there were 336 establishments in the industry, which employed 10,537 workers earning nearly $820 million in wages. Industry revenue exceeded $8.22 billion that year. Privately owned tanker numbers reached a low of 55 in 2008, a steep drop from the 454 in 1954.

At the end of the first decade of the 2000s, U.S. merchant ships engaged in the deep sea foreign transportation of freight carried more than 1 billion tons of cargo, reaching a high of $1.3 billion in 2008. The United States remained the world's largest trading nation, with export and import trade accounting for one-fourth of global trade. By far, the majority of this trade cargo was transported by ships. Nonetheless, the U.S. fleet's share of ocean-borne commercial foreign trade by weight was less than 5 percent. In 2007 the U.S. fleet ranked twelfth in the world in terms of transported tonnage and eighteenth in the number of oceangoing vessels, with its share of ocean borne commercial foreign trade by weight continuing to be less than 5 percent.

Current Conditions

Although this industry, like many others, struggled to recover from the global economic recession as the second decade of the twenty-first century began, by 2011 the outlook was fairly good. According to IBISWorld, "The overall economic revival will pave the way for industry growth, as demand for waterborne freight shipping and higher fuel prices will stimulate revenue." However, the report also noted that outside competition and high start-up costs would continue to deter industry growth.

The challenges for the U.S. shipping industry were difficult, but it was hoped that increased revenues garnered from the surge in overseas activity would provide shipping companies with the capital necessary to upgrade fleets and better prepare for international competition. Tight capacity was expected to lead to price hikes in shipping charges per container or in larger contracts when they are renegotiated.

In the early 2010s, the industry remained highly concentrated, with the top 50 companies accounting for more than 90 percent of industry revenues. Although large companies benefited in terms of port access and fleet size, small companies attempted to fill niches, such as transporting unusual cargo and working out of small ports. According to Hoover's, in 2011 the transportation of shipping containers accounted for about 55 percent of all revenues, dry bulk cargo for 15 percent, and bulk liquids and gases for 15 percent.

The remainder of the market comprised other services, such as transportation of vehicles and maintenance and repair.

Industry Leaders

In 2006 the world's largest and third-largest container carriers, Maersk Sealand and P&O Nedlloyd, respectively, joined forces under the banner Maersk. With U.S. headquarters in Madison, New Jersey, Maersk Inc. was part of Denmark-based A.P. Moeller-Maersk. The U.S. unit operated 500 container ships in 2010, which had a combined capacity of 3.4 million twenty-foot-equivalent units (TEU). Revenues for Maersk Inc. in 2010 were $205 million, and the firm employed 3,000 people.

erseas Shipholding Group, Inc. (OSG), based in New York City, was a major U.S. deep shipping firm in the early 2010s. OSG expanded in the middle of the first decade of 2000s when it acquired the 40-vessel fleet of Stelmar Shipping, Ltd. In 2007 the mpany had more than 100 international flag and U.S. flag vessels and was the second-gest publicly traded oil tanker company in the world, based on number of vessels. at year, OSG and MARAD signed the first public-private partnership under which 3G provided training opportunities for maritime academy cadets on board its ternational flag vessels. OSG posted more than $1 billion in revenue in 2010 with a orkforce of 3,500 and a fleet of 100 vessels that together had a capacity of 11 million adweight tons.

ther industry leaders included APL Ltd. of Scottsdale, Arizona, which supplied ocean ntainer transportation services through its fleet of 150 ships and 4,800 employees and corded sales of $344.7 million in 2010, and Crowley Maritime Corp. of Jacksonville, lorida. Crowley was a family-owned company, founded in 1892. By 2011 it had more an 200 vessels, 4,500 employees, and annual sales of around $1.5 billion.

esearch and Technology

oreign shipping benefited from a revolutionary improvement first introduced in omestic transport in 1956--containerization of freight as part of an integrated ansportation system. Prior to this design, cargo was lifted aboard either in separate acking crates or bundled on pallets. However, container shipping involved large ontainers that fit the chassis of a tractor-trailer that could be packed and sealed by the nanufacturer, transported via truck to the ship terminal, removed from the truck hassis, and placed in the cargo hold of the ship with a large crane that was actually part f the ship. At its destination port, the container was lifted off the ship, placed on a truck hassis, and driven to its final destination. The containers could also be hauled by train f necessary.

This innovation eliminated much of the handling that cargo once required. With this ntegrated system, it was handled once to pack it and once to unpack it, neither time by ship personnel, thus reducing the risk of damage and liability on the part of the ship owners.

Containerization also led to Ro/Ro (roll-on/roll-off) ships with their gigantic cargo doors on the sides and stern that allowed large vehicles or other large cargo to be driven or rolled on and off. Conversion to containerships was an expensive investment for ship owners, terminal operators, and port agencies. The adoption of containerships also led to the establishment of new companies that bought containers and leased them to the ship owners, relieving the ship owners of the complex problem of keeping track of the whereabouts of empty containers.

In the first decade of the 2000s, a number of shipping lines installed sophisticated computers and information technology to provide shippers with access to information about their cargo, keep track of rates, and allow customs officers to screen cargo while the ship is at sea.

In addition, many tanker companies were replacing their single-hulled tankers with double-hulled ships, which provided much better protection against oil spills and accidents. Under environmental regulations, use of single-hulled ships was originally scheduled to be phased out by 2015, but the time table was revised with restrictions.

History of Freight Transportation

Throughout the centuries there have been many modes of freight transportation. For many years, goods traveled to their destinations by way of horse drawn wagons. This mode of moving freight was slow and often dangerous. Later, with the introduction of the railway system, business owners could send goods across the country in a faster, safer way. Goods traveled to various cities via steamboat and, later, cargo ships delivered goods to foreign countries. The invention of airplanes created another option for transporting freight to faraway destinations. Business owners have always looked for better, faster, more secure ways to ship their goods. The following looks at the steady progress in the history of freight transportation.

Transporting Freight by Ship

Before the introduction of the steamboat in the early nineteenth century, many types of goods were moved by flatboat or raft. It was risky to move freight by these basic modes of transportation as well as time-consuming. In addition, flatboats, rafts, and similar watercraft had to be paddled by crew members. Steamboats transported goods in a faster, more efficient way. Today, we have cargo ships that are able to transport heavy machinery, pipes, huge rolls of wire, and even foods packed into special refrigerated compartments. In addition, there are containerships that carry cargo in large containers that can be moved easily on and off a ship. These containers may house foods, electronics or textiles along with a variety of other commercial goods.

Transporting Freight by Train

A railroad line connecting the western part of America with the eastern part was in the minds of visionaries for years. A railroad line that traveled across the entire country could transport a variety of commercial goods as well as passengers. This idea came to life in the form of the Transcontinental Railroad. In 1869, the tracks of the Union Pacific Railroad and the Central Pacific Railroad joined together to create the Transcontinental Railroad. Business owners who transported their goods across country by the Transcontinental Railroad system knew that their valuables would be secure and arrive at their destination in a timely fashion. They no longer had to depend on slow horse drawn wagons that were vulnerable to poor road conditions and other mishaps. Business owners had a better, more reliable way to deliver their goods! Today, freight trains can deliver large quantities of goods across the country. Some freight trains are made to transport raw materials such as coal and other types of minerals.

Other freight trains carry goods that need to be refrigerated such as vegetables or various dairy products. One of the biggest advantages of transporting goods by train is that this mode of transportation doesn't have to compete with cars or trucks on the road. It has its own set path all the way through to its destination!

Freight Transportation by Truck

Many types of goods travel back and forth across America by truck. Clothing, food, cars, tools, and heavy machinery are just a few examples of the commercial goods transported by trucks. During the 1930s, business owners began to deliver their goods by truck. At that time, automobiles were becoming popular and, as a consequence, the roads were being paved over and improved. The introduction of the Interstate Highway System in the mid-20th century allowed the trucking industry to experience tremendous growth. Today, trucks are responsible for a large percentage of the commercial shipping activity that occurs in the United States.

Freight Transportation by Airplane

The invention of the airplane in the early twentieth century brought forth another option in the realm of freight transportation. Over the years, improvements were made to early airplanes that eventually lead to the development of the jet. Jets and airplanes became a reliable way to transport commercial goods (cargo) such as furniture, cars, and certain types of machinery. Sometimes large animals such as horses are transported via airplane. Today, there are some airlines that provide overnight delivery of packages and letters. Delivering freight by airplane is fast and efficient though sometimes dangerous weather conditions can delay or cancel a flight. Some business owners who want their goods transported in the fastest way possible opt for delivery by air.

The glorious history of shipping

Shipping plays a very vital and significant role in today's global economy. The transportation through sea routes is considered the most economical and cheapest mode of transport, which gave rise to ship building and movement of trade by using available waterways internally for local transportation of goods and subsequently through sea for intercontinental trades. The trade has been growing steadily with each passing day from the inception and recognition of interdependence on each other's products, be it agricultural or industrial.

Countries, which are rich in raw materials and have surplus tend to export these resources to other countries, which are industrialized and able to use these materials to produce finished material by value addition and re-export to the needy countries. Likewise the countries having agro based economy, depend upon agricultural produce for export of their surplus commodities however, the countries do face a situation of trade imbalance when their imports outweigh exports by value. Pakistan is facing trade imbalance of 8 billion plus.

Over the history of shipping has witnessed various ups and downs from the very inception of this mode of transport and has undergone various technological changes. Without shipping the bulk transport of raw materials and the import / export of affordable food and manufactured goods would simply not be possible. Of all the sectors that make up the global transport infrastructure, shipping probably has the lowest public profile and the least representative public image. Today, we live in a global world, and it is certainly true that international trade among all the nations and regions of the world is nothing new. The history of the world is a history of exploration. Conquest and trade by sea.

But there is no doubt that we have now entered a new era of global interdependence from which there can be no turning back. In today's world, national boundaries offer little impediment to Multi-national Corporation. The progressive dismantling of barriers to trade and capital mobility has made the process of globalization possible. Fundamental technological advances, steadily declining costs of transport, communication and computing, its integrative logic seems inexorable, its momentum irresistible.

Looking back into history, we can trace the stages through which we have progressed to arrive at this new world order. As the world became more developed, proximity to new materials and to markets became the factors that, above all others, shaped the world's economy. In particular, the major trade patterns and shipping routes, today, international trade has evolved to the point where almost no nation can be fully self-sufficient. Every country is involved, at one level or another, in the process of selling what it produces and acquiring what it lacks: none can be dependent only on its domestic resources. Shipping has always provided the only really cost-effective method of bulk transport over any great distance, and the development of shipping and the establishment of a global system of trade have moved forward together, hand-in-hand.

The eternal triangle of producers, manufacturers and markers are brought together through shipping. This has always been the case and will remain so for the foreseeable future.

Advance in technology have also made shipping an increasingly efficient and swift method of transport. Over the last four decades, total seaborne trade has more than quadrupled, from less than 6 thousand billion ton-miles in 1995 to over 27 thousand billion ton-miles in 2004 and continues to grow steadily. In the context of a global economy, the contribution made by shipping as a major industry in its own right is very significant, and increasingly so for the developing world. Maritime activity already provides an important source of income to many developing countries indeed, developing countries now lead the world in some of shipping's most important ancillary business, including the registration of ships, the supply of sea-going manpower and ship recycling. They also play a significant part in ship owning and operating, shipbuilding and repair and port services, among others.

The history of shipping is a glorious and proud one. There is no doubt, for example, that the magnificent square riggers of the era of sail or the early 20th century's prestigious ocean liners could stir the hearts of all hose that beheld them.

But the ships of today are just as worthy of our admiration, for shipping today is in another golden age. Ships have never been so technically advanced, never been so sophisticated, never more immense, never carrier so must cargo, never been safer and never been so environmentally-friendly after introduction of engine powered ships, as they are today.

Ships are high value assets, with the larger of them costing over US $ 100/150 million to build. Ships today are modern, technologically advanced workplaces. Although general cargo ships are still largest single category, among new ships is more and more in favor of specialization for specific trades, i.e. edible/non-edible product carriers to LPG/CNG carriers. Tankers make up the second largest category. Most large modern tankers are in the 200-300,000-tonnage range. The world's largest ship today is a 564,765 dwt tanker. Bulk carriers are often called the workhorses of the international shipping fleet that typically transport commodities such as grain, coal and mineral ores.

Unheard of before the 1960s, the container is now ubiquitous and is the standard unit of cargo for just about every form of manufactured item on the planet.

Of all the sectors that make up the global transport infrastructure, shipping probably has the lowest public profile and the least representative public image. In terms of efficiency, safety, the environment and its contribution to global trade, shipping is unmatched by any other transport sector. History may be the harshest of judges but this is also true that no form of commercial transport is likely to emerge to challenge shipping as the carrier of world trade in the foreseeable future. As far as maritime security is concerned, it is appropriate to recall the words of UN Secretary General Kofi Annan in his report to the 2005 world summit: "we will not enjoy development without security, we will not enjoy security without development, and we will not either without respect for human dignity. Unless all these causes are advanced, none will succeed". Shipping affects us all. No matter where you may be in the world, if you look around you it is almost certain that you will see something that either has been or will be transported by sea, whether in the form of raw materials, components or the finished article. The sea knows no international barriers and, although most maritime enterprise takes place of sight of land, the ship is as important now as it ever was, perhaps more so. Standards of living in the industrialized and developed world, the jobs and livelihoods of billions in the developing world, all depend on ships and shipping.

The shipping industry remains the most neglected sector our economy, being 100% dependent on foreign flag vessels as far as containerized trade of over 1.8 mill teas handled at both ports and also bulk trade. Having achieved a peak of 71 Pak flag vessels of 749,046 dwt, now we are left with only 14 ships out of which 11 are nearing 30 years and that too in public sector only. Avery serious thought is necessitated by the Govt. to plan replacement of 11 public sector ship's and inducing private sector as on the pattern of India in 1980's when new ship owners were induced by, offering loan at 4%. It is not only freight bill of USD 2 bill burden on our exchequer, but we can't discount the fact that we are totally dependent on foreign lines, who can dictate us further making our impo/expo in-competitive and creating trade imbalance of over 10 bill USD. PNSC is the Last monument of Pak Merchant Marine, thus be supported, as merchant navy club has been razed to ground.

Indian fleet of 450 Vessel's 8.8 million gross tonnage is a good example of public and private sector co-operation. The shipping corporation of India (public sector) 80% Govt. owned enterprise earned a profit of 2.06 billion IRS (50.8 m USD) and owns 79 vessels, SCI has won order 18 new vessel's, is managed by shipping professionals and board comprising commercial maritime members. The chairman is optimistic to spend 3 billion USD to get 100 mark. The achievement of SCI is without any monopoly and attributed to good management and professional approach, on the contrary rejoicing turn around with monopoly and thanks to firm market with no replacement plan and new orders amounts to sullying. SCI Chairman insists on level playing field in order to compete with all players with edge on professional skills. Indian import/expo is going to touch 1 / billion tons mark in the year of 2010 compared to Pakistan 58 million tons which may touch 70/75 million tons.

I fail to understand, how any country can ignore this sector, which is the lifeline of the country. There is an old adage that "who rules the sea, rules the world". Form a think tank of professionals and business related people to suggest, how to overcome the problem of industry. There is no dearth of skilled shipping experts who may volunteer if given recognition in their country. Pakistanis have established Neptune orient line of

Singapore and Abu Dhabi Tanker Company and many more. The generalist and non-professional can't salvage the industry.

The Bottom Line...............

Let's Move Freight! – 5 Sure-Fire Tips for Freight Brokers

It indeed is a challenging job for freight brokers to build a steady stream of shippers, especially for those who are new in the industry. There are countless stories of new, enthusiastic brokers whose excitement disappeared in just a few months of customer searches while securing hardly one or two shippers.
Establishing a new business and finding customers to keep it running is always a daunting task, no matter which industry you belong to. Freight brokerage businesses aren't an exception to this. The type of services they offer may vary from other businesses, but the ways to find new customers, shippers in their case, is the same as in any other industry – with persistent doggedness and a devotion to excellence.

Following are some proven tips on how to find shippers who can bring in new business:

Target a Specific Niche

Before you start practicing as a freight broker in the truck shipping industry, it is vital to identify your niche. Once you know who your prospects are, you will better be able to build your expertise for this specific niche. Focus on a particular market will enable you to best fit your customers' needs, build strong market reputation, and stand out in the crowd.

Make Use of the Internet

Once you know who your targeted audience is, the job of finding the potential customers amongst all prospects will become a lot easier for you. One of the best ways to conduct your search is through the internet. Most of the brokers these days use the internet to find shippers and carriers in their niche.

If you are an experienced freight broker or a well-established brokerage firm, you naturally have a good exposure in the industry, and you perhaps know who are the leading shippers and carriers in your industry.

However, if that is not the case with you, there are many websites over the internet that features a complete database of all top suppliers and shippers in the country. There are several directories that even allow you to see the website URL of the respective companies and let you connect with them via email.

Be Visible on Freight Boards

Both free and paid freight boards are available out there. To get a membership on these boards, you simply need to register your company name with them. There are a large number of shippers who look out for carriers on such boards.

Free freight boards allow you to surf their database without paying a single dime. Paid boards, though, offer incentives such as a credit score – perhaps the most reliable way to confirm if a carrier or shipper is legitimate.

Making Calls Still Works!

Most freight brokers have cold feet for this tactic. But there is nothing like getting one potential customers at least out of 100 calls made to different shippers.

Often the successful callers have two traits in common: first they know why they are making a call before they call, and secondly they do comprehensive research about the company or individual they are calling.

While it's rare to get through on the first call, one should not get discouraged. Gradually with time, you will come to know what works and what doesn't. And this way you will be able to find techniques that will help you gain new shippers easily.

Make Your Presence Known Online & Offline

For creating an online presence, you can take advantage of social media platforms like Facebook, Twitter, Google-Plus and LinkedIn. And for an offline presence, it is recommended that you participate in local events, exhibitions, seminars, etc. in your trade. Staying active and ensuring on-time top-quality services to your customers at the same time will certainly gain you a loyal customer-base.

A good Freight broker program always helps greenhorn brokers learn the most effective and efficient ways of making customers, and helps them sharpen their networking skills.

Let's Move Freight – The OPERATION...............

Transportation Management Systems (TMS) is the New World of Freight Brokering.

Freight brokers who do not utilizing transportation management systems to secure capacity and manage global trade are leaving money on the table.

To be successful, as a Freight Broker you will need a TMS that not only manages rates and contracts, but also helps facilitate spot quotes across all the load boards to find capacity.

Shippers are increasingly looking at how to collaborate in private communities; carriers benefit by gaining access to customers they might not have.

Shippers are also becoming more collaborative when it comes to sharing rates, which no one wanted to do in the past. But now they understand that sharing rates helps them determine if they are not paying enough in a particular area to generate capacity.

Q: TMS solutions have reached a certain level of acceptance and maturity. What is the next level of achievement?

A: We constantly have to skate toward where the puck is going to be. For instance, shippers are looking for a single platform—a one-stop shop—to manage their supply chains. An efficient TMS enables shippers, lead logistics providers, forwarders, and brokers all to collaborate.

Traditional TMS are also bringing fleet management, driver management/pay, high-volume parcel moves, and last-mile routing into their solutions.

Q: What role does TMS play in analyzing data to enhance enterprise transformation?

A: Data plays a key role in transportation and control tower visibility, and decision support among trading partners. A TMS has to manage every piece of data, and quickly, so users can store and retrieve data in the cloud. All partners have to be able to manage the data, know when shipments are at risk, and use it to re-plan in transit.

Q: When using a TMS, what is the biggest value some shippers leave on the table?

A: Freight Brokers leave value on the table when they don't learn how to fully use a TMS. Vendor support is key. A lot of TMS training focuses on the bells and whistles, but practical application is crucial. Spend some time with your provider so you can learn how to use the TMS in your own environment to drive value.

Freight Brokers that use integrated TMS platforms can more readily and efficiently expand the services they offer to customers. A customer relationship might begin on the non-asset side of the business. Once the relationship is established, the Freight Broker may have an opportunity to move more freight through the non-asset or logistics side of its business with the customer's production goods.

Whether an order originates as a specialized flatbed load, truckload van, LTL shipment or intermodal container, an integrated TMS platform provides visibility at the enterprise level for all transactions. This visibility is essential to coordinate shipments across multiple types of equipment, lanes, modes and the use of contracted or spot market carriers.

Eventually, companies may land themselves in the position to manage all of a customer's inbound and outbound shipments. As a full-service logistics provider, they may physically touch all freight that moves through the customer's supply chain. Both inbound and outbound orders may be brought into their warehouses, staged on cross docks, and loaded onto trailers powered by company assets as well as contract carriers.

Transportation services feed off one another. As an integrated TMS platform efficiently moves orders through the system, organizations with the right visibility can identify and execute on new opportunities to grow their market share and increase profitability.

Made in United States
Orlando, FL
15 February 2024

43725419R00114